THE HEART OF SHOW BUSINESS
Your Road Map To Hollywood

BY
ALEXIA MELOCCHI
SANDI JEROME

Published by Little Studio Films

ISBN: 979-8-9919433-9-0
LCCN: 2025920114

Edited by: Heidi Stangeland
Cover by: Mark Moorer

AUTHORS NOTE

"I believe in great storytelling and that every successful artist has a deep desire to express something from the heart to create a ripple effect in our society. Emotion and entertainment are closely tied together."

A few years ago, I wrote my first book, An Insider's Secret: Mastering the Hollywood Path. I wanted to help newcomers gain invaluable insights into navigating Hollywood. I poured my heart into those pages, focusing on the insider secrets of the business of Hollywood. However, if you have been following me on social media and through my podcast, I frequently emphasize the power of mindset work and relationship capital.

Then came the year of strikes, right after we recovered from the pandemic, and the entertainment industry shut down. I started a podcast, The Heart of Show Business, and poured out my heart, encouraging others to do the same. It made its debut on the major podcast platforms worldwide, received consistent 5-star ratings, and is in the top 3% on Listen Notes.

"I was called to find a way to inspire, uplift, and educate in these very dark times. I had no idea how many would say YES to come on to my Show."

Information is power. My guests shared from Mindset to Tactics to life lessons, and took a deeper dive into how Hollywood truly works with inspirational and empowering interviews from Business Leaders and Creators around the world.

From Hollywood and beyond, my guests shared their knowledge and engaged in unique conversations on navigating Show Business and making an impact in all areas of life.

After more than 100 episodes, I have featured Oscar, Tony, and Emmy-winning talent as well as best-selling authors, successful executives, and life coaches. Some of my past guests have been actors Blair Underwood, Maeve Quinlan, Craig McGinlay, DeeDee Pfeiffer, directors Jim Fall, Jay Russell, David Winning, singer Ariana Savalas, Producer Vin Di Bona, Netflix writers Vlas and Charles Parlaplanides, and many more.

Everything I write about is from the grind and hustle and determination to become a leader in my profession, to go after my dreams with the best partner I could find: my mother.

"Alexia tells it how it is," one five-star review writes. "Not only does Alexia know her stuff, but she's also bringing a whole new level of passion and insight to what being a part of Hollywood means." And that is precisely why this book about the entertainment industry is so different from the rest; the passion and insight are unmatched. I have a seasoned perspective of the business side of the industry. But it's more than that; I put my heart into it. However, not everyone enjoys listening to podcasts or watching my popular YouTube channel. Sometimes, we enjoy the quiet moments, sitting in a park or resting at night, reading a good book. The guests I featured in this book made my heart sing, and I hope their stories have the same effect on you.

Alexia Melocchi

Contents

PART ONE

ALEXIA MELOCCHI

CHAPTER 1:
Faith, Family, and the Craft with Blair Underwood

Sometimes the universe brings the right people together at the perfect moment. My connection with Blair Underwood is one of those magical convergences. He is not only a gifted actor whose career spans film, television, and Broadway, but also someone who stepped directly into my creative orbit when he optioned CAMELOT'S COUSIN, a fascinating historical book by my client David R. Stokes. That project—about Joseph P. Kennedy Sr.'s turbulent years as U.S. Ambassador to Britain—ignited a creative chain reaction within my circle. David's earlier book had been adapted by another client, Sandi Jerome, and now David and Sandi have worked together on Sandi's remarkable family story tied to Winston Churchill, a book that was published in September. This is what a true creative community looks like—writers supporting writers, stories inspiring stories, and actors like Blair recognizing the power of bringing hidden histories to life. His involvement affirmed something I deeply believe; when you create with heart and purpose, the right partners or teammates will always find you.

And when Blair and I spoke during my podcast THE HEART OF SHOW BUSINESS, what unfolded was not just a conversation about acting—it was about faith, family, and the principles that keep a career and a life grounded.

Alexia: Blair, you're one of those rare artists who seem to live with both feet firmly planted—in your craft, your family, and your faith. Where did that artistic calling first begin for you?

Blair: Honestly, in childhood. Imagination was my playground, and I never wanted to leave it behind. Becoming other people, inhabiting different worlds. That was the spark. As actors, we "make believe," but the truth is, it's really about believing deeply.

> *"I never wanted to let go of imagination.*
> *My job as an actor is to believe so strongly*
> *that others believe too."*

Alexia: And yet you grew up in a military family—structure, discipline, responsibility. How did that shape you?

Blair: My father was an Army colonel. We were raised with duty, honor, and one clear rule: don't embarrass your father. For him to rise in the 60s and 70s as an African American officer was rare, and we carried that pride and responsibility. At the same time, my parents encouraged us to pursue our passions—if they were "legal, moral, and ethical." Ironically, both had wanted to act in their youth. So, when I said I wanted to be an actor, they not only supported me, they also became my first managers.

Alexia: You've balanced film, television, and theater, but you always return to the stage. Why?

Blair: In contrast to film and TV, where an editor shapes the rhythm, theater is purely the actor's medium. On stage, when the curtain rises, it's all you. No retakes, no filters—you live or die in front of the audience. It's terrifying, but also pure.

*"Theater is where the actor shines. You can't phone it in.
Eight shows a week—if you don't love what you do,
it will break you."*

Alexia: Over the years, what's changed most in your approach to roles and projects?

Blair: In my 20s, it was all about working nonstop, building a body of work, making mistakes, and learning. Now, I start with the script, then the character, then the people. Life's too short for unnecessary drama. Today, the process matters as much as the result.

Alexia: You've worked with legends—Ava DuVernay, Octavia Spencer, Steven Soderbergh. But I know Cicely Tyson had a special impact.

Blair: Absolutely. She was 90 when we performed THE TRIP TO BOUNTIFUL. She never missed a line, never missed a show. She did 60 push-ups every day at that age! She lived her values: health, discipline, and dignity. Working with her taught me that greatness isn't just talent, it's consistency.

*"Cicely Tyson was proof that discipline and purpose are eternal.
She never stopped giving 100%."*

Alexia: Young artists entering today's industry face both incredible opportunities and major challenges. What's your advice to them?

Blair: Believe. That may sound simple, but it's the bedrock. Your dream may not unfold exactly as you pictured it. Taking those first steps will lead you where you're meant to go. And surround yourself with the right people. Technology and inclusion have broken down old gates, but the core truth remains: your belief fuels your journey.

Alexia: You've also given back with GIVE, your Emmy-winning series about philanthropy. What drew you to that?

Blair: Service: highlighting nonprofits, children, and mental health - issues that matter beyond ourselves. The show was a win-win-win: celebrities showed their heart, charities gained exposure, and communities received real support.

Alexia: If you had to boil it all down, what are the three principles you live by?
Blair: Faith in God. Family. Work ethic. Those three anchor me in everything.

"Faith, family, and work ethic—a true trifecta."

Alexia: That's exactly why I call this THE HEART OF SHOW BUSINESS. Because it's not just about the credits—it's about the human values behind the artistry.
Blair: And kudos to you, Alexia, for giving people hope with conversations like this. At the end of the day, that's what we need most—hope.

For me, Blair Underwood represents the very best of Hollywood artistry grounded in discipline, faith anchored in purpose. His career proves that success can be built without compromising values. His journey reminds us that when imagination, integrity, and heart come together, the result is not just entertainment; it's inspiration.

KEY TAKEAWAYS

Substance over flash – Lasting star power comes from grounding your artistry in humanity, not ego.
Play the long game – Relevance is earned through thoughtful reinvention, while staying rooted in authenticity.
Lead with values – Blair shows that true success endures when it's anchored in guiding principles.

Journaling Questions

1. What are the three core principles I want to anchor my life and career in? (Blair's were faith, family, and work ethic.)

2. Where in my journey do I need to prioritize excellence over chasing recognition?

3. Who are the mentors or role models whose discipline and consistency I can learn from, as Blair learned from Cicely Tyson?

Practical Tips

- Define your compass: Write down your personal "why" for every project or goal. Ask Blair's question: *Does it uplift? Does it challenge? Does it matter?*

- Stage test: Imagine your life or career as a live performance with no retakes. What would you do differently if there were no edits?

- Excellence habit: Choose one area of your work this week and commit to Cicely Tyson–level discipline and consistency.

- Service spotlight: Identify one cause, community, or person you could use your platform or skills to uplift— even in a small way.

CHAPTER 2:
From Myth to Screen with writer Evan Spiliotopoulos

Sometimes the most meaningful connections in Hollywood don't begin in a boardroom or at a premiere—they begin with kindness. My friendship with screenwriter Evan Spiliotopoulos is proof of that. We share Greek roots, but what brought us together was something unexpected: the passing of my beloved cat, Cairo. Evan, a fellow cat lover, reached out with compassion and even joined my fundraising efforts for an animal cause in Cairo's honor. That simple act of empathy opened the door to a genuine friendship and eventually led to this conversation about storytelling, mythology, and the art of screenwriting.

Evan's career is as rich and varied as the myths he grew up with. He began writing for animation (POOH'S HEFFALUMP MOVIE, TINKER BELL AND THE LOST TREASURE) before transitioning into large-scale live-action features. His credits include THE HUNTSMAN: WINTER'S WAR, Disney's live-action BEAUTY AND THE BEAST, and CHARLIE'S ANGELS. He also ventured into darker territory with THE UNHOLY, based on James Herbert's novel, which allowed him to explore questions of faith, miracles, and corruption. This unique balance between light and dark, fairy tale and thrillers has made Evan one of the most versatile storytellers working today.

Alexia: Evan, your scripts have spanned everything from Disney fairy tales to supernatural thrillers. What unites all these different worlds for you?

Evan: Storytelling is storytelling. Whether it's a Greek myth, a biblical allegory, or a modern-day thriller, it's about characters searching for meaning. I grew up devouring myths, so I suppose I've always been drawn to big, archetypal stories that feel timeless.

> *"Mythology isn't ancient—it's eternal.*
> *Every culture has its own version, and we keep retelling them because they speak to who we are"*

Alexia: And yet, you're known for giving these familiar tales a fresh angle. How do you approach adaptation without repeating what's already been done?

Evan: By finding humanity. You respect the source material, but ask—why now? What does this story say to THIS GENERATION? With BEAUTY AND THE BEAST, for example, it wasn't about reinventing the wheel; it was about deepening character motivations, giving more emotional weight so modern audiences could connect.

Alexia: You've written for both animation and live action, for giant studios and smaller productions. Do you approach them differently?

Evan: The canvas may change, but the craft is the same. You're always asking: what does the character want, what's in their way, and what does it cost them? Animation taught me discipline— structure, clarity, rhythm. Live action gave me room to explore nuance and complexity. Both sharpened my storytelling muscles.

Alexia: You've mentioned before that your Greek heritage influences your writing. In what ways?

Evan: The Greeks invented drama—we've been obsessed with tragedy and catharsis for thousands of years. Growing up with those stories gave me a sense of scale. Even when I'm writing a thriller, I think in terms of fate, sacrifice, and redemption. It's in my DNA.

Alexia: For writers struggling to break in, what advice would you give?

Evan: . Write the story you have to tell—the one you'd regret not writing. That urgency is what will make your voice stand out.

"Don't chase trends. They'll be over by the time your script is finished."

Alexia: And on a more personal note—your act of kindness around Cairo is how we connected. How does compassion show up in your work?

Evan: Writing is empathy. You step into the skin of your characters, you feel what they feel. If you don't have compassion in life, you can't fake it on the page. That's why I value these connections—because life and art aren't separate. They feed each other.

For me, Evan Spiliotopoulos represents the storyteller as a bridge-builder—between cultures, genres, and hearts. From Beauty and the Beast to The Unholy, his work reminds us that stories are how we make sense of life. And our friendship began, fittingly, with a story of compassion, the kind that endures long after the credits roll.

KEY TAKEAWAYS

Respect the source, refresh the perspective – *Adaptation isn't about repeating what's been done; it's about asking 'Why now?' and finding the universal emotions that connect with today's audience.*

Kindness as connection – Evan's friendship and collaborations grew from simple acts of compassion, showing that human connection can spark creativity as much as any career move.

Journaling Questions

1. Which timeless themes or archetypes resonate most with me, and how can I explore them in my work?
2. Where in my projects can I deepen character motivation to make the story feel urgent and alive?
3. How can acts of empathy or kindness in my life open doors to creativity, collaboration, or meaningful connections?

Practical Tips

- **Character compass:** For each project, ask: *What does my character want? What's in their way? What does it cost them?*
- **Blend tradition and freshness:** Respect source material, but always ask: *Why now? What does this story say to this generation?*
- **Empathy practice:** Step into your characters' shoes daily. Journaling from their perspective can sharpen your understanding and emotional depth.
- **Cross-genre skill-building:** Try working in different formats (animation, live action, short form, long form) to strengthen your craft.
- **Human connection habit:** Seek out collaborations or conversations that inspire kindness, curiosity, and perspective.

CHAPTER 3:
The Magic of Believing Bigger with producer Betsy Sullenger

Some encounters stay with you because of the energy in the room. I first met Betsy Sullenger on the Disney lot, where she was working for a very well-known director of family films. From that first meeting, I admired her presence—soft yet firm, approachable yet resolute. In an industry where women are often underestimated, Betsy carried herself with the quiet authority of someone who knew her worth and wasn't afraid to take a seat at the table. I love seeing women rise within the studio system, and Betsy represents exactly that: a producer who combines grace with grit, and creativity with clear-eyed leadership.

Over the years, Betsy built a reputation for producing films that balance humor, heart, and commercial appeal. Her credits include the horror-comedy SCOUTS GUIDE TO THE ZOMBIE APOCALYPSE and the family comedy YOU AGAIN, which showcase her range in guiding projects that appeal to very different audiences. What unites her body of work is a belief that stories should entertain while still carrying an emotional truth—and that producing means being both champion and caretaker for those stories.

But Betsy didn't stop there. After her studio years, she made the bold pivot into independent producing—a leap that required an entirely different skill set. Suddenly, there wasn't a studio safety net. She had to navigate financing, build teams from scratch, and champion projects without the cushion of big budgets or established pipelines. Indie producing, she told me, demands creativity not just on-screen, but in every logistical decision. It's a tougher road, but one that gave her greater freedom to back projects she truly believed in.

Alexia: Betsy, you've worked within the studio system, which can be both thrilling and challenging. What first drew you to producing?

Betsy: Producing felt natural to me because I've always loved being part of the whole process—finding a story, developing it, supporting the talent, and seeing it through. It's about shaping a vision and then bringing the right people together to make it real.

Alexia: When we first met at Disney, I remember being struck by your calm but firm energy. Do you see that as part of your producing style?

Betsy: You're the one people turn to when things get chaotic. If you stay calm, you give everyone else permission to breathe and focus. At the same time, you have to hold the line when it comes to the vision—you can't let it get diluted.

"A producer has to be both anchor and compass."

Alexia: You've navigated a system that hasn't always been easy for women. How did you find your way?

Betsy: I learned to trust my instincts and my preparation. Hollywood can be intimidating, but if you know your material and respect the people you're working with, you'll earn respect in return. And I think it's important to lead by example—firm when needed, but also kind.

Alexia: After your studio films, you made the leap into indie producing. How was that transition?

Betsy: Night and day. In the studio system, you have resources, departments, and infrastructure. In indie, you wear ten hats, and every decision counts toward whether the film actually gets made. It was harder in many ways—but also liberating. I could back stories that mattered to me personally and learn every facet of the business.

Alexia: What's the most important lesson you've learned about producing?

Betsy: The producer's job is to create the conditions for everyone else to shine, from the director to the cast to the crew. When you get that right, the film takes on a life of its own.

"That it's not about control, it's about collaboration."

Alexia: And what advice would you give to the next generation of women producers?

Betsy: Don't try to mimic anyone else's style. Lean into your own strengths, even if they're not what Hollywood traditionally celebrates. Authenticity builds trust—and trust builds careers.

For me, Betsy Sullenger embodies the kind of producer Hollywood needs more of a leader who balances strength with grace, authority with compassion. With credits like You Again and Scouts Guide To The Zombie Apocalypse, she has shown her versatility inside the studio system. And with her pivot to indie production, she proved that courage, resilience, and heart can light the way even when resources are scarce. Betsy reminds us that the heart of show business isn't just in the stories we tell—it's in the determination to keep telling them, no matter the obstacles.

KEY TAKEAWAYS

Soft Power, Strong Vision – Betsy Sullenger shows that true producing blends calm authority with clear-eyed leadership. Success comes not from control, but from creating conditions where everyone else can shine.
Balance is everything – Strength and grace, grit and empathy: Betsy proves that versatility and resilience are as important as talent and experience.
Courage fuels growth – From studio films to independent producing, taking calculated risks allows you to champion projects that truly matter.

Journaling Questions

1. Where in my career or creative work could I bring calm authority like Betsy—anchoring others while keeping vision clear?

2. What strengths are uniquely mine, and how can I lean into them instead of mimicking others?

3. When have I taken a risk that required learning new skills, and what did it teach me about resilience?

CHAPTER 4:
Behind the Lens with director Jim Fall

Some collaborations are born out of timing, others out of shared passion. My connection with director Jim Fall came from both. Years ago, we were developing a teenage film centered around Duran Duran fandom, a story close to my heart, and one that Jim was the perfect fit for. Not only was he a fan of the music himself, but he had already proven his gift for directing broad, family-friendly teen movies with LIZZIE MCGUIRE. The band loved him, the energy was right, and it felt like the stars were aligning.

Then the Writers Guild strike happened. The project stalled, as so many did in that turbulent time, and ultimately never came to be. But while the movie didn't happen, the connection endured. Jim and I have remained friends and collaborators at heart, always on the lookout for the perfect project to bring our creative energies together again. That kind of enduring creative chemistry is rare in Hollywood, and it speaks volumes about who Jim is—not just as a director, but as a person.

Jim's career reflects the same qualities I first admired in him: warmth, and an instinct for stories that connect across generations. He first broke out with TRICK, a groundbreaking romantic comedy that was one of the first mainstream gay love stories told with joy and lightness instead of tragedy. He went on to direct THE LIZZIE MCGUIRE MOVIE, which became a cultural touchstone for an entire generation. Later, he brought his signature charm to television with HOLIDAY ENGAGEMENT and THE WEDDING MARCH. Across indie and studio, rom-com and family comedy, Jim has proven himself as a filmmaker who can blend humor with heart and always capture the spirit of the moment.

Alexia: Jim, you've directed both independent films and studio projects. What draws you to a story?

Jim: Whether it's a teen comedy or a love story, I want to feel like these are real people audiences can root for. If I care about them, the audience will too.

"Characters first."

Alexia: TRICK was such a groundbreaking film in its time, and LIZZIE MCGUIRE became a cultural touchstone. What connects those experiences for you?

Jim: They seem so different, but for me, both were about capturing a specific cultural moment with honesty. TRICK was about telling a gay love story without tragedy attached—just joy, awkwardness, and romance. LIZZIE MCGUIRE was about giving kids a voice and celebrating the messy, funny parts of growing up. Different audiences, same idea: tell the truth, and people will see themselves in it.

Alexia: When we first spoke about the Duran Duran project, it felt like such a perfect fit. How did your love of music shape you as a director?

Jim: Music is an emotional shorthand. A song can tell you more about a character's feelings than dialogue sometimes can. Being a fan myself—of Duran Duran, of 80s pop—it's in my DNA to use music as a storytelling tool. That's why that project felt so exciting. And though it didn't happen then, who knows? There's always another opportunity down the road.

"Hollywood is full of stop-and-start stories."

Alexia: . How do you stay inspired when projects fall apart?
Jim: You remember why you started in the first place. We don't do this because it's easy—we do it because we love it. Every setback is temporary. What lasts are the relationships and the next idea that keeps you up at night.

"Don't wait for permission."

Alexia: What advice would you give to young directors today?
Jim: . Make something, even if it's small. The tools are more accessible than ever. And surround yourself with collaborators who get you—because filmmaking is a team sport.

For me, Jim Fall represents the best of creative partnership: kind, strong, and very passionate about stories that inspire and connect people. He is also a bit of a rebel, and I love rebels.
And one day soon, I know we'll find that perfect project to make together.

KEY TAKEAWAYS

Capture the cultural moment – From *Trick* to *Lizzie McGuire*, honesty in depicting life—big or small—resonates across generations.
Creative chemistry endures – Relationships and collaboration often outlast projects. Trusting and nurturing those connections is as vital as the work itself.

Journaling Questions

1. Where in my projects can I focus on creating characters audiences will truly root for?
2. How can I use my personal passions (music, culture, hobbies) as storytelling tools?

CHAPTER 5:
Winning with Stillness
with NFL athlete Keith Mitchell

Some of the most transformative stories come to us from unexpected places. I met Keith Mitchell through the publisher of EDEN MAGAZINE, where I was a regular contributor. At the time, I didn't consider myself very sports savvy—football was a world far removed from my own. But when I learned Keith's story, I was deeply inspired. Once a celebrated NFL linebacker, his career ended suddenly with a spinal injury. What could have been a devastating conclusion became the beginning of an extraordinary new chapter: his journey into yoga, mindfulness, and breathwork.

Keith's turning point began in a hospital bed. One moment, he was a powerful athlete at the peak of his career; the next, he was paralysed, unable to move without pain. The silence of that room forced him to confront himself. Stripped of the identity of "football player," he had to discover who he was without the game. It was there, in the stillness, that he first connected to his breath—one inhale and one exhale at a time. Those early moments of conscious breathing became the foundation of his healing.

What moved me most was not just Keith's physical recovery but the way he transformed his pain into purpose. Through breathwork, meditation, and yoga, he rebuilt his body—and more importantly, discovered a mission to help others reclaim their own health and inner peace. Today, Keith is a teacher, speaker, and healer who has shared his practices with veterans, first responders, underserved communities, and even corporate leaders seeking balance in high-pressure environments.

Alexia: Keith, your transition from NFL athlete to yoga teacher is extraordinary. How did that shift even begin?

Keith: It began in the hospital. I was flat on my back, paralysed, and all I had was my breath. At first, I didn't even know I was "practicing"—I was just trying to survive. But each inhale and exhale calmed me, gave me strength. That's when I realized the body has its own intelligence.

"Breath was the bridge back to myself."

Alexia: Many people would have been crushed by such a career-ending injury. What gave you strength?

Keith: At first, I WAS crushed. My identity was tied to football. But in losing that, I discovered something deeper—my spirit. I realized I wasn't just an athlete; I was a human being with a purpose beyond the game.

"When you lose what you thought defined you,
you finally discover who you really are."

Alexia: You now teach breathwork and yoga to people from all walks of life. What do you see as the most powerful aspect of these practices?

Keith: Breath is universal. We all have it, and yet we overlook it. Conscious breathing resets the nervous system, calms the mind, and begins to heal the body. It's the simplest, most accessible tool we have—and it's always with us.

Alexia: What's the biggest misconception people have about yoga and meditation?

Keith: That it's about flexibility or sitting perfectly still. It's not. It's about presence. It's about learning to listen to your body and quiet the noise. You don't need to be a yogi on Instagram to benefit. You just need to start with one breath.

Alexia: You often talk about service. Why is that so central to your path now?

Keith: Because healing isn't just for me. Once you've walked through something hard and found a way forward, you owe it to others to share. Service turns suffering into something meaningful.

For me, Keith Mitchell is proof that reinvention is possible at any moment of our lives. From the roar of the stadium to the stillness of the hospital bed, and finally to the peace of the yoga mat, he embodies resilience, presence, and purpose. His journey reminds us that true strength is not measured in trophies or titles—it's measured in how we breathe, heal, and show up for others.

KEY TAKEAWAYS

Loss as a doorway – When identity tied to achievement is stripped away, new purpose can emerge. Keith's journey reminds us that endings can be beginnings in disguise.

Service amplifies healing – Turning personal struggle into tools for others magnifies impact and meaning. Breathwork, mindfulness, and compassion become vehicles for change.

Journaling Questions

1. When have I experienced a sudden shift that forced me to reconsider who I am?

2. What practices—breath, meditation, movement, reflection—help me reconnect to myself in moments of challenge?
3. How can I transform my own struggles into service that benefits others?

Practical Tips

- **Breath first:** Start each day with conscious breathing—five minutes of awareness can reset your nervous system and focus your mind.
- **Redefine identity:** Reflect on areas where you tie your self-worth to a single role or achievement. Ask: *Who am I beyond this?*
- **Start small:** Healing doesn't require perfection. Begin with one breath, one movement, or one moment of stillness.

CHAPTER 6:
The Cabaret Queen
with performer Ariana Savalas

Some stories are even more inspiring when you've witnessed the transformation firsthand. I first met Ariana Savalas through a friend of her father, the legendary actor Telly Savalas. We were invited to see her perform. At the time, she was a very shy teenage girl—sweet, reserved, and singing other people's songs. Even then, there was a spark. But what I could not have imagined then was how that spark would grow into a full fire.

Over the years, Ariana evolved into a true force of nature. She began writing her own music, experimenting with performance styles, and eventually stepping boldly into cabaret. She became a founding member of the wildly popular Postmodern Jukebox, reimagining hit songs with vintage flair and performing on some of the world's most iconic stages—from Radio City Music Hall in New York, to the Greek Theatre in Los Angeles, to grand halls in Vienna, Singapore, and London. A multi-instrumentalist—she plays piano, percussion, and is especially known for her ukulele—Ariana combines musicianship with theatricality. Today, she stands as a musical burlesque queen, a mistress of the modern Moulin Rouge, fusing cabaret, rock and roll, and comedy into a one-of-a-kind stage persona that is fearless, playful, and magnetic.

"Cabaret is freedom. It's storytelling without rules."

Alexia: Ariana, when I first saw you perform, you were this quiet teenage girl singing covers. How did you make the leap into becoming the cabaret powerhouse you are today?
Ariana: I had to find my voice—literally and figuratively. At first, it felt safer to sing other people's hits. But there came a moment when I knew I couldn't keep hiding behind that. Writing my own music and embracing cabaret let me express all the parts of myself—wild, romantic, funny, even outrageous.

Alexia: Cabaret is such a unique choice, blending music, theatre, and burlesque. What drew you there?
Ariana: . I can be glamorous one moment, comedic the next, heartbreaking the next. It's not about perfection, it's about connection. And honestly, it's fun to shock people a little.

Alexia: Your father, Telly Savalas, was such an iconic figure. How has his legacy influenced you?
Ariana: He was larger than life, unapologetic, and authentic. He taught me not to be afraid of being bold. Even though he's not here, I feel his presence every time I step on stage. I think he'd love the mischief in what I do.

Alexia: You once described yourself as a "romantic realist." Can you explain what that means?
Ariana: It means I believe in magic, but I'm also grounded. I know bubbles burst, fame fades, but while the glitter lasts, you should revel in it. And then? You create new glitter.

"Embrace the awkwardness. Lean into it."

Alexia: What advice would you give to young performers who are still shy or unsure of themselves?
Ariana: . The more you perform, the braver you get. And

remember—perfection is boring. People connect with honesty, not polish.

For me, Ariana Savalas is living proof that artistry is an act of courage. Her journey is a reminder that we don't find our voices overnight—we build them, word by word, song by song, performance by performance. Let's dare to dazzle, and above all, to be unapologetically ourselves.

KEY TAKEAWAYS

Find your voice, then own it – Ariana's leap from shy cover singer to global cabaret star reminds us that growth happens when we step into our unique creative identity, even when it feels risky. **Connection over perfection** – Whether through music, theatre, or performance, audiences respond to honesty, presence, and joy more than polish.

Journaling Questions
1. In what ways am I hiding behind what feels safe, rather than expressing my full creative self?
2. How can I lean into my "awkwardness" or imperfections to strengthen my authenticity?
3. What elements of my artistry allow me to connect deeply with others, and how can I amplify them?

Practical Tips
- **Performance bravery:** Take small creative risks daily—experiment with style, tone, or medium to stretch your range.
- **Play and mischief:** Infuse joy, humor, and surprise into your work—it strengthens engagement and personal expression.

CHAPTER 7:
The Business of Story
with Sales Agent Michael Favelle

Over the years, Michael Favelle and I have crossed paths at countless film markets — AFM, MIPCOM, Cannes — always weaving business with friendship. Markets can be exhausting, but Michael's sharp sense of humor, deep knowledge of the industry, and unwavering camaraderie always made them feel more like reunions than obligations.

One of the most special gestures he extended to me was his YEARLY invitation to watch the Red-Carpet arrivals at the Cannes Film Festival from his office, which had the perfect view overlooking the Palais. For a newcomer, that would be a pinch-me moment. For me, it was something deeper — an acknowledgment that years of hard work, persistence, and authentic networking led to privileges like this. Sitting there, looking down at the parade of stars and gowns, I felt lucky — but also reminded that luck is often the byproduct of dedication and trust.

When I first connected with Michael, I immediately recognized him as someone who thinks globally, not just locally. In an era where content is consumed everywhere, by everyone, Michael's expertise in international markets is invaluable. He's a dealmaker who doesn't just see the film — he sees the audience and knows how to bridge the two. What I admire most is his candour about the business mechanics that so many creatives either overlook or avoid.

Alexia: Michael, you've been in the trenches of global film sales for years. What's the number one mistake you see filmmakers making when it comes to distribution?

Michael: It's not. Making the film is the starting line. If you don't know who your audience is, what your marketing strategy is, or how your film will travel internationally, you've already handicapped your project. The business side is not optional — it's the oxygen for your creativity.

> *"Too many filmmakers still think that making the film is the finish line."*

Alexia: That's something I emphasize constantly. And yet, so many creatives resist the business side. Why do you think that is?

Michael: Because it's not sexy. Everyone loves the glamour of the premiere, but no one talks about recoupment waterfalls, MGs (minimum guarantees), or territorial rights. But here's the thing: if you want a career, you have to learn it. Otherwise, you'll always be at the mercy of people who know more than you do — and that's dangerous.

Alexia: Exactly. So, what does success look like in today's marketplace?

Michael: Success is adaptability. Streamers have changed the landscape, audience habits have shifted, and budgets are under more scrutiny than ever. The filmmakers who win are the ones who know how to pivot. Maybe your project starts as a feature but becomes a limited series. Maybe your financing comes from unexpected territory. If you're rigid, you'll break. If you're flexible, you'll thrive.

> *"The biggest mistake I see is over-pitching."*

Alexia: Since so many of our readers attend film markets and festivals, what's your advice when it comes to pitching?

Michael:. Creators feel they need to tell me their whole life story and every detail of their project in one sitting. That doesn't work in a market where everyone is running from one meeting to the next. What does work? Clarity and brevity. Tell me the title, the hook, and why an audience will pay to watch it. Then stop. If I want more, I'll ask.

The other thing: don't insult your buyer by saying your project is 'for everyone.

And finally — don't hand me a script in the hallway. Ever. That's the fastest way to lose credibility.

> *"Nothing is for everyone. If you can't articulate your target market in one sentence, you're not ready to pitch."*

Michael is a straight shooter, which is why I value his voice so much. He reminds filmmakers — and even seasoned producers — that the dream doesn't end at "Fade Out." Hollywood is a business, and international distribution is a huge part of that.

Michael's insistence on adaptability — and his tough-love advice on pitching — is pure gold. He's right: if you don't know your market, if you can't communicate your story clearly, you're not building a career, you're gambling with it.

KEY TAKEAWAYS

Know your audience – Michael emphasizes that making a film is just the starting line. Understanding who will watch it, why, and how it will travel internationally is crucial.

Adaptability is key – Markets, platforms, and audience habits change constantly. Flexibility in format, financing, or strategy separates those who thrive from those who falter.

Clarity over over-explaining – A concise, focused pitch communicates professionalism and respect for your audience. Overloading details or claiming your project is "for everyone" undermines credibility.

Journaling Questions

1. How well do I understand my audience and the path my work will take beyond creation?

2. When I pitch my work, am I clear, concise, and compelling—or do I risk over-explaining?

Practical Tips

- **Audience map:** Before launching a project, define your ideal viewers and why they'll care.
- **Pitch practice:** Summarize your project in one sentence for the hook, one for the target audience, and one for the emotional payoff. Stop there—let curiosity do the rest.
- **Adaptability habit:** Identify one area where flexibility could improve your project's chances—format, financing, or distribution—and experiment with alternatives.
- **Relationship building:** Invest in genuine connections at festivals and markets; these often matter more than immediate deals.

CHAPTER 8:
The Guardian of Nature
with environmental advocate Andrea
Crosta

I first met Andrea Crosta at an environmental advocacy event hosted by Better Earth Media. As an Italian myself, I felt an immediate kinship with him, but what truly drew me in was his mission. Andrea is the founder of **Earth League International**, a nonprofit dedicated to fighting environmental crime and wildlife trafficking. For those of you who know me, you'll understand why I couldn't resist inviting him to my podcast, THE HEART OF SHOW BUSINESS. My love for animals and wildlife conservation runs deep, and Andrea's work touched me profoundly.

Andrea has an unusual background for an environmental activist. Before founding Earth League International, he spent years as a business and security consultant. He has used that same investigative expertise to fight some of the most insidious crimes threatening our planet today — from illegal logging and fishing to the multibillion-dollar trade in endangered species. His team works much like an intelligence agency, embedding undercover operatives, building trust with insiders, and running long-term investigations. Through **whistleblowing networks**, traffickers are exposed, their operations documented, and their names delivered to authorities who can take action.

His work is not just theoretical — it has been featured in global media and even spotlighted in the **Netflix** documentary THE IVORY GAME, which brought worldwide attention to the dark underbelly of elephant poaching and ivory trafficking. Andrea doesn't just talk about saving the planet; he builds cases that bring criminals to justice.

Alexia: Andrea, you come from the world of intelligence and security, and you've applied those skills to environmental protection. What made you decide to take that leap?

Andrea: I realized that the same organized crime structures behind drugs, weapons, and human trafficking were also behind wildlife crime. And nobody was really paying attention. The environmental world was full of passion but often lacked the tools, methods, and discipline of intelligence work. So, I thought, "Why not bring those worlds together? If we don't treat environmental crime as a serious crime, we will always lose.

Alexia: That is so powerful. Many people still think of conservation as something romantic, like saving elephants or protecting rainforests. But you've said it's really a crime problem. Why do you frame it that way?

Andrea: Because it IS a crime. If we just talk about conservation as charity, we miss the point. These are crimes against humanity because when ecosystems collapse, we all suffer. So, we need to fight them like any other major criminal enterprise — with intelligence, undercover work, whistleblowers, and international cooperation.

> *"We're talking about mafia-style networks making billions of dollars off destroying our natural world."*

Alexia: And for people reading this — filmmakers, artists, entrepreneurs — who want to help but don't know how, what's the first step?

"Educate yourself. Don't look away."

Andrea: Start by understanding the scope of the problem. Then use your skills. If you're a storyteller, tell stories that raise awareness. If you're an entrepreneur, think about how your work impacts the environment. Everyone has a role. This isn't someone else's problem — it's all of ours.

"Conservation is not charity —
it's a battle against organized crime."

Like many of you, I grew up loving animals and believing conservation was about passion, empathy, and activism. Andrea doesn't take away from that, but he reframes it — showing that the fight for wildlife is also the fight against corruption, organized crime, and greed.

What fascinated me most was the behind-the-scenes reality of his work. He and his team risk their lives by infiltrating trafficking networks, collecting intelligence, and building whistleblowing pipelines that governments often cannot create on their own.

Meeting Andrea reminded me that the heart of show business is not only about entertaining audiences but about inspiring them to care, to act, and to imagine a better world.

KEY TAKEAWAYS

Fight with strategy, not just sentiment – Andrea reframes environmental protection as a crime-fighting mission. Passion alone isn't enough; rigorous methods, intelligence work, and accountability are critical.

Use your skills for impact – Whether you're a storyteller, entrepreneur, or artist, everyone can contribute. Your platform, creativity, or expertise can raise awareness, change behaviours, and hold perpetrators accountable.

Storytelling as a force for good – Media, film, and art can expose hidden truths and inspire action. Andrea's work shows that stories aren't just entertainment—they can mobilize, educate, and protect.

Journaling Questions

1. In what ways can I use my skills or platform to address problems I care about?

2. How can I combine passion with strategy to make a real difference in my field or community?

3. Are there areas where I've overlooked systemic issues that require disciplined, persistent action?

Practical Tips

- **Educate first:** Understand the problem deeply before attempting solutions—research, follow experts, and seek firsthand accounts.

- **Leverage your platform:** Whether through storytelling, social media, or business, use your influence to amplify urgent issues.

- **Identify actionable steps:** Small, consistent actions—donations, campaigns, collaborations—compound into meaningful impact.

- **Think like a strategist:** Approach challenges with method and foresight, just as Andrea uses intelligence techniques in environmental advocacy.

CHAPTER 9:
The Ocean's Voice
with explorer
Jean-Michel Cousteau

I first met Jean-Michel Cousteau when I had the privilege of interviewing him for the cover of EDEN MAGAZINE. From the moment our conversation began, I felt the depth of his legacy. As the son of the legendary Jacques Cousteau, Jean-Michel inherited not only his father's pioneering spirit but also his passion for protecting the ocean. Yet what struck me most was how he has made that mission uniquely his own.

Our interview took on an unexpected warmth because we spoke in French — a language I am fluent in, and one that immediately created a sense of camaraderie and cultural connection. It was a pinch-me moment, not only because I was speaking with an icon, but also because one of my all-time favorite films has always been THE BIG BLUE.

Jean-Michel has spent his life exploring and advocating for the seas, not just as a filmmaker and environmentalist but as an educator determined to awaken the next generation. Through the **Ocean Futures Society**, he has carried forward the Cousteau name with a vision that blends science, adventure, and storytelling. His documentaries and advocacy work remind us that the ocean is not a resource to exploit, but a living system we depend on for survival.

Alexia: Jean-Michel, you grew up with one of the greatest explorers in history as your father. How did you find your own path in his shadow?

Jean-Michel: My father opened the door to the ocean for me, but I had to decide how I would walk through it. For me, it was about education. Exploration is important, but if people don't understand why the ocean matters to their daily lives, they won't protect it. So, I focused on teaching through films, lectures, and direct outreach.

"Every second breath we take comes from the ocean."

Alexia: You often speak about the ocean as the "life support system of the planet." Can you explain what you mean?

Jean-Michel: n. It regulates our climate, provides food for billions, and holds solutions we are only beginning to discover. When we destroy it, we destroy ourselves. When we protect it, we protect our future.

Alexia: And for the artists, storytellers, and entrepreneurs reading this — how can they contribute to ocean advocacy?

Jean-Michel: Use your gifts. If you are a storyteller, show the beauty of the ocean and the dangers it faces. If you are a business leader, look at how your decisions impact the sea. Everyone has a responsibility. We cannot leave it to scientists alone — we need culture, creativity, and compassion to inspire change.

Speaking with Jean-Michel was like speaking with history and the future all at once. He carries the weight of a family legacy that changed how we see the planet, yet his focus is not on the past but on the generations to come.

Our French conversation made the interview feel like two friends sharing not just words but a worldview — tied together by culture, language, and the deep respect we both hold for the sea.

Films, stories, and interviews can shift perspectives, ignite empathy, and inspire action. And when I think about show business at its best, it is exactly this: entertainment that awakens responsibility.

KEY TAKEAWAYS

Lead with purpose, not pedigree – Jean-Michel took the legacy of his father and made it his own, focusing on education and storytelling to engage people in ocean conservation.

The ocean is life support – Every breath, every meal, and every climate system depends on the seas. Protecting them isn't optional—it's essential.

Creativity as a catalyst for change – Art, film, and storytelling can awaken responsibility, shift perspectives, and mobilize communities to act.

Journaling Questions

1. How can I use my talents—storytelling, art, or business skills—to make a positive environmental impact?

2. Where might I be relying too heavily on experts and neglecting my own ability to influence change?

Practical Tips

- **Integrate action into creativity:** Use your projects—films, articles, campaigns—as platforms for awareness and advocacy.

- **Think long-term:** Legacy-building requires sustained effort; focus on initiatives that have enduring impact.

- **Collaborate across disciplines:** Scientists, artists, and business leaders all have roles to play; seek partnerships that amplify impact.

CHAPTER 10:
The Brothers who brought Gods to life with screenwriters Charles & Vlas Parlaplanides

Some stories are too epic to stay on the page. The Parlaplanides brothers took the myths of their Greek heritage and reimagined them for a global audience, bringing ancient gods, heroes, and monsters into the bold, stylized world of anime. Their Greek heritage gives their work a unique flavor, one that often blends myth and fantasy

Our connection began in a deeply personal way — through the **Los Angeles Greek Film Festival**, where I served on the Board, and through the shared community of our church, **Saint Sophia Cathedral**. As fellow Greeks in Hollywood, there was an instant bond. We spoke the same cultural language, one rooted in story, faith, and tradition, and that foundation has carried into our friendship ever since.

The brothers first broke into Hollywood with the feature film IMMORTALS, an epic tale inspired by Greek mythology that starred Henry Cavill, Mickey Rourke, and Freida Pinto. It put their names on the map as writers who could bring larger-than-life stories to the big screen. But their journey didn't stop there.

Recently, they took a bold step into a new and groundbreaking space: **anime for Netflix**. Their hit series BLOOD OF ZEUS REIMAGINED Greek mythology through the lens of Japanese animation, proving that great storytelling can transcend mediums and cultures. The show quickly gained a global following, praised for its epic battles, striking visuals, and deeply human characters.

Alexia: What made you want to become writers?

Charles & Vlas:
"We didn't grow up in Los Angeles. Hollywood felt a million miles away. But stories? Stories were always with us. We used to sit around, talking about ideas, bouncing characters off each other, and it became this shared language between us."

Alexia: Hollywood is filled with solo writers trying to make their mark. What's the advantage of being a writing team?
Charles & Vlas: Screenwriting is already such a lonely process. Having a partner means you have someone to celebrate with when things work, and someone to lean on when they don't. We push each other to go further, to find the better idea, the sharper line, the truer moment. It keeps us honest — and it keeps the work fun.

Alexia: Your Netflix anime series BLOOD OF ZEUS became an international success. What was that journey like?
Charles & Vlas: It was liberating. Anime doesn't have the same limitations as live action — the only boundaries are your imagination. It allowed us to lean into our love of myth, epic battles, and larger-than-life characters. And because it was Netflix, the story instantly had a global platform. For two Greek American brothers to bring the tales we grew up with to millions around the world — it was a dream come true.

"Writing isn't about waiting for the muse. That's the biggest myth. We wrote every single day, no matter what."

Alexia: Many writers struggle with moments where the blank page feels impossible. What do you do when you just can't come

up with something to write?
Charles & Vlas: We step away. Go live life. Watch a movie. Take a walk. Travel. Inspiration rarely strikes when you're forcing it — it comes when you're open. The worst thing a writer can do is punish themselves for being blocked. Sometimes your brain just needs to refill. The trick is: don't stop being curious. Pay attention to the world. When the well is refilled, you'll be ready.

The Parlaplanides brothers remind me that in show business, collaboration can be a superpower. Watching them build worlds together, refine dialogue, and lean into their heritage makes me think of my own journey — how identity and culture shape the stories we tell.

KEY TAKEAWAYS

Collaboration as a superpower – Writing with a partner pushes ideas further, keeps the work honest, and turns a lonely process into a shared adventure.
Heritage informs imagination – Greek mythology shaped their storytelling, proving that cultural roots can be a wellspring for universal stories.
Step away to refuel – Creativity isn't forced. Sometimes the best ideas come when you live life, explore, and stay curious.

Journaling Questions

1. Who are the collaborators or mentors who help you elevate your work, and how can you deepen those partnerships?

2. How does your cultural or personal heritage influence the stories you tell?

3. When I feel blocked, what life experiences or observations can help me refill my creative well?

Practical Tips

- **Honor your roots:** Identify the elements of your background, culture, or personal experiences that enrich your storytelling.

- **Give your mind space:** Step away from work when stuck. Walk, travel, or immerse yourself in different art forms to reignite inspiration.

- **Experiment with mediums:** Don't be afraid to translate your stories into new formats—animation, podcasting, or digital platforms can expand your reach.

CHAPTER 11:
The Power of a Bold Choice
with Director Katt Shea

I first met Kat Shea years ago at the Peninsula Hotel in Beverly Hills. We were both circling a movie project that, like many in Hollywood, never came to fruition. But something far more enduring came out of that meeting — a connection that lived on through social media. What kept us bonded was our shared love of animals. Horses, dogs, rescues — we would always find ourselves sharing stories or cheering each other on in the little acts of compassion that matter.

For years, I thought of Kat as the fearless director of dark, edgy material. But when she came on my podcast, she surprised me. She wanted me to know that her heart had shifted. She is now committed to family films, uplifting stories, and inspiration, because the world desperately needs that right now. That conversation lit up a path for us to not only reconnect but also dream up a special project we'll be working on together.

Alexia: Kat, your story is so unique — you began as an actress, yet you carved out your place as a director. What made you want to step behind the camera?
Kat: Honestly, it started when I was a kid in Michigan. I was writing plays and charging parents to come see their kids perform in my backyard. (Laughs) I guess it was always in my

DNA. But the real turning point came when I started working with Roger Corman. I stumbled into second-unit shooting, kept saying yes to opportunities, and one day I pitched him a movie about strippers. I didn't even plan to direct it, but suddenly I blurted out, "And I'll direct it!" That became STRIP TO KILL.

"I didn't plan to direct it.
But I found myself blurting out, 'and I'll direct it!'"

Alexia: Roger Corman once called you the woman who could make a $500,000 movie look like $10 million. That's both a compliment and a challenge, right?
Kat: *(Laughs)* Oh, definitely both. Roger tested me by cutting budgets and schedules in half, just to see if I could still pull it off. It made me tough, resourceful, and fearless. That foundation gave me the confidence to direct POISON IVY, which ended up changing Drew Barrymore's career and my own.

"Your heart is the key to art,
to connection, to everything."

Alexia: And what's beautiful is that your body of work has evolved. You began with edgy thrillers but later shifted to more family-oriented films like NANCY DREW and RESCUED BY RUBY for Netflix. Was that a conscious pivot?
Kat: Absolutely. In the beginning, what sold were risqué, edgy stories. But my real passion has always been in finding the unexpected good. The strippers in STRIP TO KILL weren't tawdry — they were frustrated artists, performance artists. Over time, I realized I wanted to bring more light into the world. Working on RUBY every day was nourishing to my soul.

"At this stage of my life, I don't want to add more darkness to
people's lives. I want to make movies that uplift and heal."

Alexia: That sense of compassion also extends to your advocacy for animals.

Kat: Always. I've rescued horses, fostered dogs — animals are healers. On set, they light up when they get attention and purpose. They're performers, too. And honestly, the love they bring is the same love I want audiences to feel when they watch my films.

> *"Even the animals love the attention.*
> *They're performers too."*

Alexia: You also coach actors. From your perspective as a director, what makes you say "yes" to a role?

Kat: It's all about the arc. Actors crave transformation. If a character starts one way and ends another — that's irresistible. Even a small role can be powerful if there's a shift.

> *"Without an arc, there's no magic."*

Alexia: You've said your spiritual practice, NATURAL WAY OF LIVING, keeps your heart centered. How does that translate into your work?

Kat: It's about opening your heart and letting love guide you, instead of ego. That's not easy, but it changes everything. It makes me a better director, teacher, and human being. At the end of the day, your heart is the key to art, to connection, to everything.

Kat Shea's career is a story of reinvention, courage, and love. From outsmarting Roger Corman on shoestring budgets to inspiring audiences with heartfelt films on Netflix, she has proven that a woman's voice behind the camera brings both toughness and tenderness. She began by spotlighting artistry in the unlikeliest of places — the strip club stage — and continues to illuminate the beauty of transformation, whether in actors, animals, or audiences.

For me, reconnecting with Kat after all these years feels like a full-circle moment. She's no longer just the director who knows how to shock and provoke; she's the storyteller who wants to heal and inspire.

KEY TAKEAWAYS

.

Reinvention is possible at any stage – Kat pivoted from edgy thrillers to uplifting family films, showing that your creative path can evolve without losing authenticity.
Resourcefulness breeds confidence – Early challenges and tight budgets taught her resilience, problem-solving, and fearless leadership.
Empathy extends beyond humans – Animals, like actors, bring joy and connection. Compassion in small actions translates to larger storytelling impact.

Journaling Questions
1. How can I let heart and empathy guide my work without compromising vision or standards?
2. In what areas of my career or creative life could I embrace reinvention or a new direction?
3. What challenges have taught me resilience, resourcefulness, and confidence that I can carry forward?

Practical Tips
- **Follow your curiosity:** Say yes to opportunities that challenge you, even if they push you out of your comfort zone.
- **Spot transformation:** Seek stories or projects with character arcs or evolution — change creates connection.

- **Lead with love, not ego:** Decisions guided by heart inspire trust, collaboration, and authenticity..
- **Celebrate reinvention:** Don't be afraid to pivot your creative focus or audience; evolution is part of a lasting career.

CHAPTER 12:
Keeping Bernie Alive (and Hollywood too) with actor Jonathan Silverman

Jonathan Silverman is one of those rare actors who has lived the Hollywood dream — starring in hits like WEEKEND AT BERNIE'S — and yet managed to remain grounded, steady, and genuinely kind. When I interviewed him, what struck me most wasn't just his career longevity but the mindset that carried him through decades of highs, lows, auditions, and reinventions. t's funny how life has a way of coming full circle.

Jonathan came into my life through our mutual friend, actress Maeve Quinlan, a close friend of mine who thought he would be the perfect co-lead for a Christmas movie we were developing. What makes it even more serendipitous is that *Weekend at Bernie's*—the film that made Jonathan a household name—was one of the very first titles I ever bought on behalf of my Italian distributors when I was just starting out as a young sales agent in the business. Back then, I couldn't have imagined that one day I would be considering him as a collaborator on one of my own projects.

That's the magic of Hollywood: it's a circle, sometimes small, sometimes vast, but always spinning back to connect you with people and projects in unexpected ways.

"Rejection is part of the deal."

Alexia: You've had such a long and diverse career, from beloved comedies to guest spots on countless shows. What's the mindset that's allowed you to sustain your career over the years?
Jonathan: I always tell people:

"Don't burn too hot and don't go too cold. Stay lukewarm. "

That means not letting the highs carry you away or the lows bury you. There will be joys and successes, but there will also be disappointments and failures. The one constant has to be that you love what you're doing. If you love it, you'll keep going no matter what.

Alexia: That's such a refreshing perspective. What about dealing with rejection? Every actor and creative faces it constantly.
Jonathan: You can't take it personally, or at least you can't let it stay personal. Sometimes you weren't right for the role, sometimes it was politics, sometimes it was timing. If you get too wrapped up in it, you'll burn out. That's why 'lukewarm' works — it keeps you steady.

Alexia: So much wisdom in that. If you could go back and tell your younger self something when you were just starting out, what would it be?
Jonathan: Enjoy the ride more. I was always focused on the next thing, the next audition, the next break. Looking back, I wish I had stopped more often to just appreciate where I was, even when things weren't perfect. Because truthfully, the journey itself is the reward.

Jonathan's philosophy hit me hard because it's so opposite of the frantic energy we often glorify in Hollywood. He's not saying don't care. He's saying care deeply but also protect your energy.

That balance — that "lukewarm" state — is how you keep loving the work without letting the work consume you.

I also love how Jonathan reframes rejection. For so many creatives, rejection feels like a verdict. For Jonathan, it's just part of the process — and not a reflection of your worth.

And his reminder to ENJOY THE RIDE? That one stayed with me. So often, we creatives are so focused on climbing that we forget to look around at the view.

KEY TAKEAWAYS

Love the journey – Career longevity comes from enjoying the process, not obsessing over the next audition, break, or milestone.

Detach from rejection – Setbacks are part of the work, not a reflection of your worth. Emotional steadiness keeps creativity alive.

Consistency beats intensity – Steady, genuine effort sustains a career far better than bursts of extreme highs and lows.

Journaling Questions

1. Where in my life or career could I adopt a "lukewarm" approach to protect my energy and maintain balance?

2. How can I reframe rejection or disappointment as part of the journey rather than a personal verdict?

3. What moments or experiences am I overlooking because I'm too focused on what comes next?

Practical Tips

- **Anchor in your passion:** Identify what you genuinely love about your craft and let that guide your focus, rather than external validation.

- **Pause and reflect:** Take moments to appreciate your progress, even in the midst of setbacks or routine.

- **Set emotional boundaries:** Don't let wins inflate your ego or losses crush your motivation — steady emotional management sustains creativity.

- **Steady practice:** Build routines, habits, and rhythms that allow you to show up consistently without burning out.

CHAPTER 13:
The Inner Glow
with actress Sofia Milos

Sofia Milos is a citizen of the world—born in Switzerland, half Greek, half Italian, and fluent in several languages. Many know her as CSI: Miami's detective, or as the formidable mafia boss on THE SOPRANOS. But what makes Sofia unforgettable is not just her resume; it's her essence: a blend of strength, sensitivity, and artistry.

We bonded quickly—maybe because we're rare in Hollywood: two women with the same Mediterranean roots, who can switch languages mid-sentence. But beyond that, I connected with Sofia because she embodies what THE HEART OF SHOW BUSINESS is all about: inner beauty fuelling outer creation.

Alexia: You once described yourself as having "the persistence of a warrior" but also "the sensitivity of a child." That moved me. How did you come to that self-definition?
Sofia: I left home very early, and I was blessed—and cursed—to see different realities and cultures. My immigrant parents wanted me to live a proper, structured life. When I chose acting, my father especially couldn't accept it. To him, being an artist was almost indistinguishable from being a sinner. Over time, though, as he saw me on TV, he realized the discipline and work behind it.

Alexia: Yet you didn't just rely on luck. You studied for years at the Beverly Hills Playhouse with Milton Katselas.

Sofia: Yes, for over a decade. He taught us discipline. You showed up sick or well, because art is a responsibility. He said society runs on dreams, and it's the artist's job to communicate them. Later, I studied with Ivana Chubbuck, who helped me sharpen how to communicate more efficiently as an actor. Different teachers, different gifts, but all about responsibility in the craft.

"Passion. Curiosity. Childlike."

Alexia: I know you've gone on a deep journey of self-development. Was there a moment when you decided, "I need to understand myself more"?
Sofia: From my teens, I knew life was bigger than just the name or the place I was given. I used to journal on napkins, even toilet paper, or anything. Knowledge is power, yes, but only if you use it. That's why I work on my mindset daily. It's like a muscle; whether through meditation, prayer, reading, or reflection, I strengthen it so I can make conscious choices

Alexia: One thing I admire about you is how you celebrate other women. That's rare in Hollywood.
Sofia: Thank you. I believe jealousy comes from unaddressed insecurities. Strong women inspire me: Sophia Loren, Lucille Ball, Katharine Hepburn. They were rebels, warriors, yet deeply feminine. I think women are extraordinary: we embody nuance, beauty, detail, and sensitivity. We complement men—we don't compete.

*"When women support one another, we don't just shine
— we illuminate."*

Alexia: Many women look at you and wonder, "How does she stay so radiant and strong?" What's your secret?

Sofia: Mindset first. Then consistency. I work out four to seven days a week, sometimes a walk on the beach, sometimes power yoga, sometimes swimming. I eat clean, don't drink, don't smoke. Passion is also key. If you don't feed your passion, you age. Goals fuel passion. Without them, life shrinks.

Alexia: Define yourself in three words.
Sofia: Passion. Curiosity. Childlike.

What struck me most about Sofia Milos is that discipline and artistry are not opposites but partners. Whether it was showing up to class no matter what at the Beverly Hills Playhouse or treating mindset like a muscle that must be trained daily, Sofia reframes success as responsibility—to yourself, and to the dreams you're entrusted to communicate.

KEY TAKEAWAYS
Discipline as responsibility – Consistency in your craft (showing up, training, learning) is a form of honoring your work and the dreams you communicate.
Mindset is a muscle – Daily reflection, meditation, journaling, and study keep your choices conscious and intentional.
Celebrate, don't compete – True power comes from uplifting others, especially women, and recognizing complementary strengths rather than rivalry.

Journaling Questions
1. How can I balance persistence and sensitivity in my own creative or professional life?
2. What daily practices strengthen my mindset and focus, like Sofia's approach to "training the muscle"?
3. Who inspires me, and how can I celebrate their strengths instead of comparing myself?

Practical Tips

- **Consistency matters:** Show up to your craft daily, even when motivation fluctuates.
- **Mindset practice:** Dedicate time for meditation, journaling, or reflection to strengthen mental clarity.
- **Celebrate others:** Look for opportunities to lift peers, mentors, and colleagues — generosity breeds collaboration.
- **Physical + mental synergy:** Regular movement, clean eating, and rest support both energy and creativity.
- **Curiosity and childlike wonder:** Approach life and work with openness; ask questions, explore, and experiment.

CHAPTER 14:
Oxygen for the Soul with Breathwork Guru Jon Paul Crimi

Some encounters are not about the "business" part of show business, but about the HEART of it. Meeting Jon Paul Crimi was one of those encounters. Our paths crossed through the wellness and creative communities in Los Angeles. Jon Paul is a former addict who turned into a transformational breathwork facilitator who has guided thousands of people, including Hollywood A-listers, musicians, athletes, and everyday seekers, into unlocking their own healing and creativity through the power of breath.

What struck me most was his raw honesty. He is not the typical "wellness guru." He's blunt, authentic, and has lived through enough darkness to speak from experience. He will tell you that he was a bouncer at Hollywood clubs, an actor in movies you've probably seen, and a man who lost his way—before finding purpose in guiding others.

I had heard whispers about his breathwork sessions: that they were so powerful, even grown men would break down in tears as years of buried emotion came rushing out. Curious, I signed up for one of his classes in Los Angeles. What happened next was nothing short of extraordinary. In the middle of the session, I found myself sobbing uncontrollably—and not even embarrassed about it. It was a release I didn't know I needed. His work, raw and unpolished, bypasses the mind and cuts straight into the heart. No wonder so many celebrities—like Matthew

McConaughey, Halle Berry, and musicians seeking to clear stage anxiety—show up when he rarely teaches in LA.

"You can't fake breath. You just show up, do it, and it cracks you open."

In an industry that demands constant performance, resilience, and reinvention, artists often carry invisible weights—fear of failure, rejection, self-criticism, childhood wounds. Breathwork is not about thinking your way out of those blocks; it's about breathing your way through them. As Jon Paul often explains, the breath bypasses the intellect and goes straight into the body, dislodging what's been stuck for years.

For actors, this means accessing deeper emotional truth in their craft. For singers, it frees the voice from the tension of unprocessed pain. For writers and creators, it clears the mental fog and reignites inspiration. Simply put, breathwork is like clearing out the emotional hard drive, so new creativity can flow without interference.

Alexia: Why breathwork? Why not another healing modality?
Jon Paul: Because it works. You can't fake breath. You show up, you do it, and it cracks you open. You don't need to believe in it, you just need to do it.

Alexia: What happens in those moments when people—like me—just start sobbing in the middle of class?
Jon Paul: That's the body letting go of what the mind has been holding onto. And when it leaves, people feel lighter, freer, more themselves.

"Trauma, grief, self-judgment—it gets stuck.
Breath shakes it loose."

Alexia: Why do you think so many celebrities and artists seek you out?

Jon Paul: Because art demands truth. If you're blocked emotionally, it shows up in your work. Breathwork strips away the lies you tell yourself and leaves you with raw authenticity. That's what great performances and great art come from.

Alexia: what's the biggest takeaway you want people to leave with after a session?

Jon Paul: That healing isn't about perfection. It's about being real. The more real you are with yourself, the more you can connect with others—and that's where the magic in art and life comes from.

Try This: A 2-Minute Breathwork Reset

Jon Paul often says you don't need a full session to feel the shift—just two minutes of conscious breathing can change your state:

1. Sit or lie down comfortably.

2. Place one hand on your belly and one on your chest.

3. Inhale deeply **through the mouth**, first filling the belly, then the chest.

4. Exhale **through the mouth** with a sigh or sound.

5. Continue this circular breath—inhale belly, inhale chest, exhale mouth—without pausing in between.

6. Try it for two minutes. Notice if emotions, tingling, or energy arise. Let it flow without judgment.

It's a simple exercise, but it's a glimpse into the powerful work Jon Paul brings into people's lives.

KEY TAKEAWAYS

Authenticity over perfection – Healing and artistry are not about achieving an ideal state; they are about being real, fully present, and vulnerable.

Creativity unlocked – Breathwork frees expression for actors, singers, writers, and all creators by clearing emotional and mental clutter. True art emerges from authenticity.

Power of showing up – The process isn't about belief—it's about participation. Showing up to your practice, even briefly, triggers transformation.

Journaling Questions

1. What emotional blocks or fears might I be holding onto that affect my creativity or personal life?

2. How can I incorporate moments of conscious breathing to reset and reconnect with myself?

3. Where in my life am I prioritizing perfection over authenticity? How can I shift toward realness?

4. When was the last time I allowed myself to release emotion fully without judgment?

Practical Tips

- **Two-minute reset:** Practice circular breath—inhale belly → inhale chest → exhale mouth—for 2 minutes. Notice physical sensations, emotions, or energy shifts.

- **Use breath for creativity:** Before writing, performing, or problem-solving, do a few conscious breaths to clear your "emotional hard drive."

- **Embrace vulnerability:** Allow yourself to feel fully without censoring or controlling, both in art and in life.

CHAPTER 15:
Identified Possibility with actress Dee Dee Pfeiffer

Some interviews feel like catching up with an old friend. When I connected with actress Dee Dee Pfeiffer, I was struck by her candour and warmth. Dee Dee, the younger sister of Michelle Pfeiffer, carved her own path in Hollywood with roles in beloved shows like CYBILL, FRIENDS, ER, and, most recently, as Denise Brisbane on ABC's BIG SKY. But what makes her story powerful is not just her résumé; it's her resilience.

From the very start of our Zoom conversation, I felt an instant bond with her. She laughed as she told me how she travels across America for shoots with all her animals in tow— including a cockatoo. That detail said everything about who she is: grounded, nurturing, and unapologetically herself.

Dee Dee is also a recovering alcoholic. She has been open about her sobriety journey and the courage it takes to rebuild not only a career, but a sense of self. In Hollywood, where image often hides pain, her honesty is a gift. She didn't sugarcoat the struggle. Instead, she spoke about falling down, getting back up, and learning to live a life anchored in gratitude and service.

Alexia: You've had incredible roles across tv and film, but you've also been very open about your personal battles. What was the turning point for you?

Dee Dee: The turning point was when I realized I couldn't keep hiding. Addiction had taken me to a dark place, and the hardest part was admitting it — not just to others, but to myself. That honesty was terrifying, but it was also the doorway to my freedom.

"I had to stop pretending everything was fine."

Alexia: That's such a powerful statement. How did you find the courage to step into that new chapter?

Dee Dee: I call it becoming an "identified possibility." Once I understood that I wasn't just broken but actually filled with potential — everything shifted. I began to see my struggles not as shameful, but as my greatest training ground. I realized I could use my journey to help others. That gave my pain purpose.

Alexia: what role has acting played in your recovery and transformation?

Dee Dee: Acting is storytelling, and storytelling is healing. I can channel my wounds into characters and make them real. That vulnerability isn't a weakness — it's a superpower. When you've lived through fire, you bring authenticity to the screen that no amount of technique can teach.

Alexia: how does sobriety influence your work on set today?

Dee Dee: I show up present. I show up grateful. I don't need to escape anymore—I use my truth. That's what connects with audiences, not some polished version of me.

Alexia: what advice would you give to others in the business struggling with addiction or self-doubt?

Dee Dee: Don't isolate. Talk to someone. Ask for help. You're not alone—even if Hollywood sometimes makes you feel that way.

"Sobriety is like opening your hand. When it's clenched, nothing new can come in. But when you open it, life can place possibility right there."

Try This: Becoming an "Identified Possibility"

Dee Dee's words invite us to shift perspective. Instead of seeing yourself as "broken" or defined by setbacks, ask: WHAT IF THIS IS MY TRAINING GROUND? WHAT IF THIS PAIN IS PREPARING ME FOR SOMETHING GREATER?

Take a moment to reflect:

1. Write down one struggle you've faced that still carries weight.

2. Next to it, write down one skill, lesson, or strength that came from surviving it.

3. Imagine yourself as an "identified possibility"—not limited by your past but expanded by it.

It's a small exercise, but it's the first step in reframing your story the way Dee Dee has reframed hers: as a source of authenticity, power, and freedom.

Speaking with Dee Dee reminded me that the heart of show business is not found in the bright lights or the red carpets, but in the resilience of those who keep creating despite life's storms.

KEY TAKEAWAYS

Becoming an "identified possibility" – Reframing setbacks as training grounds allows personal pain to transform into purpose.

Instead of hiding or shaming struggles, see them as opportunities for growth, skill-building, and helping others.

Presence over perfection – Sobriety and self-awareness create a grounded approach to work and life. Showing up fully present and using your truth connects with people far more than polished façades.

Connection is key – Healing and growth thrive in community. Asking for help and sharing experiences prevents isolation and fosters empathy, both personally and professionally.

Journaling Questions

1. What struggle or setback in my life still carries weight?

2. How has that experience shaped a strength, skill, or insight I now possess?

3. In what ways can I use my personal journey to help or inspire others?

4. How can I show up more authentically in my work or relationships today?

Practical Tips

- **Reframe your story:** Write down one struggle and next to it, note the growth, lesson, or strength it produced. Visualize yourself as an "identified possibility."

- **Presence practice:** Before work or creative projects, take a moment to center yourself, acknowledge your truth, and set an intention to show up fully.

- **Gratitude reflection:** End each day noting one thing you are grateful for, reinforcing presence and grounding.

CHAPTER 16:
Fighting for the Underdog with director Dimitris Logothetis

Some conversations remind you why you fell in love with storytelling in the first place. When I sat down with director and producer Dimitri Logothetis—the creative force behind *Kickboxer, Jiu Jitsu,* and most recently *Gunner* with Morgan Freeman and Luke Hemsworth—I was struck by how seamlessly his life mirrors the themes of his films.

An immigrant, a martial artist, and a multi-hyphenate storyteller, Dimitri carries himself with the same loyalty, respect, and honor he brings to the screen. Behind the action and spectacle is a man who believes discipline is freedom, and that stories aren't just entertainment—they're a way of passing down values that endure.

Alexia: You've worked with some of the most iconic action stars in the world. Why action and martial arts?
Dimitri: The action is just the obstacle. Family, loyalty, and doing the right thing. Those are the values that drive them. Martial arts shaped me too: respect, loyalty, honor. That core finds its way into every story i tell.

> *"What really interests me are characters up against impossible odds — people who should lose but choose to fight because they have a code."*

Alexia: Those qualities — respect, honor, loyalty — aren't always what Hollywood is known for.

Dimitri: That's why i write underdogs. I came here at six years old. My dad was a mechanic; people told me I'd never make it. But I thought, why not me? My father said, "nobody's better than you, nobody's smarter than you. But don't ever think you're better than anyone else." That stuck. It's the immigrant spirit — resilience, humility, persistence.

"My characters don't live with compromise. When something terrible happens, they act. They do the right thing — what we all wish we could do."

Alexia: You've been a writer, director, and producer. Which came first?

Dimitri: Writing. Always writing. Storytelling was my way through school. Even Marty Scorsese once grabbed a paper out of my hands on set and told me, "You're a good writer — go to film school." Producing came later because, frankly, if i didn't produce, i couldn't hire myself. And directing — that was born of necessity and trust. At the end of the day, I call myself a filmmaker because it's all connected.

Alexia: What's the secret to longevity in this business?

Dimitri: Persistence. And trust. Actors sign on when they trust the director and the team. Buyers back what they know they can sell. And audiences just want to be entertained. There's no magic formula. You do your best, deliver heart, and keep swinging.

"Why not you? Nobody's smarter than you. Nobody's better than you. You have the right to succeed."

Alexia: And when life knocks you down?

Dimitri: I learned from the greatest fighters in the world: Ali, Frazier, Foreman. When you get knocked down, you don't stay down. Get off the mat, take a breath, and get back in the ring. Success isn't about avoiding failure. It's about refusing to quit.

> *"Get up off the mat. Take a deep breath.*
> *Start swinging again."*

Dimitri reminds us that action movies aren't just explosions and fight scenes — they're morality tales, modern myths where character still matters. His underdogs mirror our own battles: to be seen, to belong, to fight for what we love. And like the fighters he's filmed and admired, he lives by the simplest, hardest truth: GETTING BACK UP.

KEY TAKEAWAYS

Persistence and resilience – From immigrant roots to Hollywood, Dimitri emphasizes that success is about showing up, keeping trust, and refusing to quit. Life knocks everyone down; what matters is the choice to rise again.

Storytelling as legacy – Writing, producing, and directing are tools to convey enduring values. Dimitri treats films as modern morality tales, reflecting real-world struggles and inspiring audiences to fight for what matters.

Trust and relationships – Longevity comes from building trust with collaborators, actors, and audiences. People back those who are reliable, authentic, and committed to the craft.

Journaling Questions

1. In what areas of my life or work am I practicing resilience?

2. What personal values do I want to reflect in my work or creative output?

3. When have I faced setbacks, and how did I respond? How could I approach similar challenges differently?

Practical Tips

- **Define your code:** List 3–5 personal or professional values that guide your decisions. Revisit them before starting any project.

- **Persistence practice:** When faced with a setback, write down one concrete action to "get back on the mat." Then take it immediately.

- **Storytelling with heart:** Identify the underlying message or moral in your creative work. Ask, "What enduring values am I passing on?"

- **Learn from the underdog:** Study people or characters who overcame adversity; note strategies you can apply to your own challenges.

CHAPTER 17:
Blissipline and the Heart of Now with Reverend Michael Beckwith

Some encounters feel less like an interview and more like stepping into a higher vibration. Sitting with Reverend Michael Beckwith, founder of the Agape International Spiritual Center and a voice that touched millions through *The Secret*, I was struck by the way he carries wisdom like music. Each sentence flowed with rhythm, equal parts sermon and jazz riff.

He spoke of presence, love, and harmony not as distant ideals, but as daily practices that can tune the soul and reshape how we live.

Alexia: How did Rhonda Byrne find you for THE SECRET?
Rev. Beckwith: It was pure serendipity. She had a layover in Los Angeles came to Agape, heard me speak, and ran up afterward asking if I'd be in her movie. The next day, i was filming on a green screen. That moment changed everything. People still come up to me around the world who've just discovered it.

"True artists live on the edge of creativity.
At Agape, they feel the same urgency and surrender.
It's a camaraderie in creativity."

Alexia: Everyone says, "I'm spiritual." But what does that mean to you?
Rev. Beckwith: Spiritual means eternal. We are spiritual beings, whether we know it or not. Parents don't create us — they allow

us into this dimension. Our real self emerges from eternal presence.

> *"We're not flawed beings trying to become perfect; we're perfect beings unfolding."*

Alexia: Why is music and dance such a part of your ministry?
Rev. Beckwith: Music is vibration. Since we are 80–90% water, sound literally changes our chemistry — it lifts our immune system, slows aging, *and* dissolves disease conditions. Add dance, and people move their bodies into joy. Real music isn't entertainment; it's entrainment into *a* higher frequency.

Alexia: Fear has been called the real virus of our times. How do we overcome it?
Rev. Beckwith: You don't get rid of fear — you transmute it. Fear becomes excitement, excitement becomes enthusiasm. Walk in the direction of your vision, and fear turns into fuel.

> *"Discipline comes from being a disciple of what you love. When you love the practice — meditation, affirmation, visioning — it stops feeling like homework. It becomes a 'blissipline.' you don't leave home without it."*

Alexia: What do you feel when you lead retreats in nature?
Rev. Beckwith: Trees are alive. They literally bow vibrationally to your divinity. The forest is our second set of lungs. When we awaken spiritually, reverence for nature follows. You don't pollute what you love.

> *"The tree recognizes your divinity — even when you forget it."*

Alexia: Many empaths feel overwhelmed by the world's pain. How do we protect ourselves?
Rev. Beckwith: Instead of absorbing everything, radiate. Feel

your way into love, peace, or joy, then bring that into the room. Don't be a vacuum cleaner. Be the light.

"Justice without love is revenge.
Only love can build a world worth living in."

Reverend Beckwith reminded me that spirituality is not about polishing flaws away, it's about unfolding into wholeness.

Most of all, he reframed empathy: it is not about absorbing the world's pain but radiating enough light to transform it. In the end, he taught me that the HEART OF SHOW BUSINESS — and the heart of life — is to become an instrument tuned to love, joy, and presence.

KEY TAKEAWAYS

Blissipline – Discipline becomes effortless when it is rooted in love and joy. Meditation, affirmation, and visioning are practices you carry naturally, not chores.

Fear as fuel – Fear is not the enemy; it is potential energy. When directed, it transforms into excitement, enthusiasm, and action.

Empathy reimagined – Protect yourself by radiating light rather than absorbing pain. Your energy can uplift and transform without being depleted.

Music, movement, and vibration – Sound and motion are tools for elevating consciousness, healing the body, and creating joy. Creativity thrives in this flow.

Journaling Questions

1. Which practices—meditation, affirmation, breathwork— bring you the most joy and presence?

2. How do you currently respond to fear? How could you transform it into energy and action?

3. Where do you feel drained by others' energy? How could you shift from absorbing to radiating?

4. How does music, movement, or nature affect your mental, emotional, or creative state?

Practical Tips

- **Daily Blissipline:** Pick one practice you love (meditation, journaling, music, yoga) and do it consistently for 10–20 minutes daily.

- **Fear Fuel Exercise:** Identify a current fear, then write one small action step you can take toward it. Reframe fear as excitement.

- **Radiate, don't absorb:** When interacting with stress or negativity, imagine sending out calm, love, or joy rather than taking it in.

- **Nature connection:** Spend at least 10 minutes a day outside, noticing the trees, sounds, and life around you. Reflect on how it energizes you.

- **Creativity tuning:** Incorporate music, dance, or rhythm into your workday to enhance focus, flow, and joy.

- **Connection with nature** – Trees, forests, and natural surroundings respond to reverence. Spiritual awakening fosters care, respect, and love for the environment.

CHAPTER 18:
Money, Love & the Unfolding Self with comedian Kyle Cease

Too many in Hollywood chase the cup: the next credit, the next deal, the next applause. But the real power is in remembering we're the waterfall, the source, not the container. That's the heart of show business

When I call something my "go-to," I mean it's dog-eared and coffee-stained. Kyle Cease's THE ILLUSION OF MONEY is exactly that for me, equal parts mindset reset and practical compass. He's a comedian turned transformational teacher who refuses to trade truth for polish. Which, let's be real, is why he's here.

Alexia: You started as a stand-up phenom—then wrote THE ILLUSION OF MONEY. Let's debunk the "starving artist" myth. What changed?
Kyle: I grew up in entertainment—my uncle worked with Gallagher, my grandma puppeteered on THE CAROL BURNETT SHOW. I was headlining clubs at 18, movies at 20. And still, I lived inside a lie: "When something happens, I'll be happy." Book the movie → need the next movie. It never ends. The pivot was this: "When I'm truly okay, things happen." I began letting go of what felt heavy—addictive foods, booze, even gigs that weren't aligned. Space opened. A new career emerged: comedy +

transformation, theatres like the Dolby, two books. I moved from ACHIEVING (forcing a known outcome) to UNFOLDING (allowing what I can't yet see).

"An acorn can't see the forest inside it.
Unfolding beats achieving."

Alexia: I've noticed money and love carry the same obsessive energy, enough when we have it, everything when we don't. Your line hits: "Your obsession with money is costing you millions." Why do we chase these to feel we matter?

Kyle: Because we start under the illusion that we DON'T matter. Here's a truer sentence: Every dollar you ever made came from you. You're the waterfall; money is a cup you filled. If I show you the cup, you hoard. If I show you the waterfall, you share. Make YOU the source again. Same with love: stop outsourcing your worth to a partner or a crowd. Be the love you're hunting, and you'll meet people doing the same inner work. Otherwise, it's two addictions holding each other up.

"You're bigger than money
—you're the source that created it."

Alexia: Artists feel called to help—to make beautiful work, to save the proverbial 100 dogs. Then rent shows up. How do we honor a big calling without being trapped by it?

Kyle: First, check if your "calling" is actually powered by old wounds. A lot of "I must change the world" is "so I'm not a failure / unloved." Life blocks those ego-missions on purpose. Real callings arrive one present step at a time: forgive here, say no there, host THIS event. Less five-year plan, more daily obedience.

"Many 'callings' are costumes our trauma wears.
Truth gives you the next step—not a two-year plan."

Alexia: After the pandemic, I expected more compassion. Instead: volatility. Why?

Kyle: Because it's healing. Anger surfacing beats denial, smiling. Identities— "achiever," "victim," "brand"—are dissolving. What's suicidal isn't YOU; it's a pattern trying to die. Let it. Sit. Meditate. Drop the addictive scroll. Control-based systems are failing, so surrender can lead.

> *"What's dying is not you—it's the lie about you."*

Hard medicine, but it lands. The industry isn't ending; the pretending is.

Alexia: You're also a dad. How do you parent without shutting down that inner guidance?

Kyle: Boundaries for safety, freedom for soul. Seatbelt is non-negotiable. The HOW she wears it—her choice. I model authenticity in real time, so she learns she isn't her patterns; she's the presence noticing them.

> *We talk a lot about "hustle." Kyle quietly replaces*
> *it with "honesty." Different h-word, different life.*

Alexia: I say life is made of moments—we remember the scene, not always the plot. So...what's your next moment?

Kyle: Honestly, there is no "Kyle" to plan around. The more I sit in silence, the more old identities purge and new ideas arise. My job is frequency over output. If higher consciousness quietly reforms millions, that beats a billion books from a lower state.

> *"I'd rather be a higher frequency doing nothing*
> *than a lower frequency doing everything."*

Alexia: What do you want people to expect when they see you live?

Kyle: No pedestals. I'm willing to be messy, scared, honest—so what's false can leave. We're all works-in-progress. If someone looks perfect on Instagram, that's brand management, not enlightenment.

Alexia: Final tradition: three words that define you, or your life mantra.
Kyle: All. That. Is. We're not separate. The assignment is oneness.

> *"You are not next to the universe*
> *—you are made of it."*

 Talking with Kyle Cease reminded me why his work resonates so deeply. Too many in Hollywood chase the cup—the next deal, the next applause—forgetting they're the waterfall itself. Kyle flips the script: success isn't about achieving, it's about unfolding. He shows how money, love, and even "purpose" can become addictions if we outsource our worth. The medicine he offers is radical honesty—letting go of false callings, dissolving old identities, and choosing presence over performance. His reminder stays with me: you're not chasing the source—you are the source.

KEY TAKEAWAYS

You are the source – Money, love, and validation are cups we fill. Obsessing over them keeps us chasing rather than creating. Remember: you are the waterfall; the world receives what you naturally generate.
Callings vs. ego costumes – Many "big missions" are actually old wounds in disguise. The real work comes in present, daily steps—saying yes, saying no, forgiving, showing up—rather than chasing a five-year plan.

Journaling Questions
1. What areas of your life feel like "cups" you're chasing? How could you shift focus to being the "waterfall"?

2. Which parts of your "calling" are authentic vs. ego-driven? What is the next small step toward truth?
3. Where are you holding onto old identities or patterns that no longer serve you?
4. How can you prioritize presence, frequency, or alignment over output and hustle?
5. When have you allowed messiness or vulnerability to create connection or growth?

Practical Tips

- **Daily unfolding:** Identify one thing you can do today that aligns with your truth, without obsessing over long-term results.
- **Presence reset:** Spend 10 minutes in silence, meditation, or conscious breathing. Notice how it shifts energy, ideas, or perspective.
- **Frequency over output exercise:** Pick one task today and approach it with full presence, letting go of urgency. Notice the quality vs. quantity impact.
- **Radical honesty** – Surrendering false identities, patterns, and societal expectations creates freedom. Let the "lie about you" die and allow your true presence to guide action.
- **Frequency over output** – Your energy, presence, and inner alignment matter more than constant hustle or visible achievement. Being a higher frequency shifts the world more than busy work from a lower state.
- **Parenting with authenticity** – Model presence and inner guidance, not patterns or ego. Safety + freedom allows others (and yourself) to navigate life consciously.
- **Messiness is growth** – Showing up as a work-in-progress allows others to shed pretenses. Perfection is a social media illusion, not enlightenment.

CHAPTER 19:
The Art of Living on Purpose with Michael Nitti and Erica Nitti

I first invited Michael Nitti onto my own battlefield: film markets. As I spiraled about competition and getting into the right rooms, he smiled and said, "Put on your magician panties." Translation: choose your archetype and walk in on purpose. That two-millimeter shift changed my whole festival. Today, Michael and his daughter/co-author Erica Nicole Nitti bring their mastery framework to artists and entrepreneurs who want certainty without losing heart.

> *"Mastery isn't a place you get to; it's a place you come from—on purpose." — Michael*

Alexia: Michael, give us the quick heartbeat of *The Trophy Effect* and your archetypes.

Michael: We're animals with a survival brain scanning for danger. Left unchecked, it makes us reactive—careful instead of bold. Mastery is noticing that voice, thanking it for its entertainment value, and choosing who you'll be on purpose. Archetypes are practical doors into that choice—two masculine, two feminine energies. You need access to all, and the intuition to shift between them. Most of us under-use the Magician. Choose it on purpose, then go make magic.

> *"Certainty is a practice, not a personality trait." — Erica*

Alexia: Erica, what was it like growing up with a coach-dad?

Erica: I wasn't intimidated—I was independent (and a little rebel). The defining moment was at twelve when he asked, "Is this how you want to feel?" I realized I could observe my mind and choose differently. Later a near-death car accident clarified my purpose - be the light and show the light.

Alexia: Creatives are emotional. How do you teach "mastery" without shutting feelings down?

Michael: You don't shut them down—you wield them. Bring full emotion when you act, pitch, or write, then keep living on purpose when the director says "cut." Mastery isn't a sterile state; it's an intentional one.

Erica: Creatives are brilliant at turning emotions on for the work—then judge themselves off-camera. The inner critic rides shotgun. We teach them to expect that voice, dance with it, and stay intentional anyway.

Alexia: What about the "what if they don't like it?" voice?

Erica: It shows up every time I level up. Now it's a signal I'm growing. Anticipate it, play with it, and keep going.

Michael: Doubt isn't truth; it's biology. Bring excellence anyway. If it doesn't land, recalibrate and bring more. Certainty is a practice.

Alexia: How does coaching extend the book?

Michael: Like a sports coach, we hold your hand while you run plays in life—feedback, reps, accountability, excellence.

Erica: And we provide a safe, honest space to be vulnerable, claim your patterns, and operationalize intention daily.

Alexia: One quick compass for turbulent times?

Erica: Breathe. Slow down. Be curious. Listen to understand.

Michael: Lead with outcome and empathy, not volume. Intend the greater good—and remember no one wakes up to be "the enemy."

*"Why would you ever show up as anything
less than awesome?"* — Michael

✦ *Talking with Michael Nitti reminded me why his wisdom cuts
through the noise. In a world obsessed with being in the "right
room," he teaches that mastery isn't something you achieve—it's
something you choose, on purpose. With Erica Nicole Nitti at his
side, their framework reveals that certainty isn't about control,
but about practice, how doubt is a biological phenomenon—not a
truth—and how our archetypes are doors into the power we
already possess. Michael calls us to stop performing for approval
and start creating from intention. Erica reminds us that the inner
critic is just proof we're stretching. Together, they offer a radical
compass for artists and entrepreneurs alike: don't chase
validation—choose who you are, then go make magic.*

KEY TAKEAWAYS

Emotions = Fuel: Channel feelings into the work and the room—
then choose your state between takes.
Certainty is Trained: Doubt will ride along. You drive.
Excellence Everywhere: Reps at the grocery store count. Lead
with acknowledgment and intention in every micro-interaction.
Two-Millimeter Shifts: Small energetic adjustments (voice,
posture, intention) change outcomes disproportionately.
Outcome Over Opinion: In conflict, anchor to the result you want
for the greater good.

Journaling Questions

1. **Spot the Survival Script:** Where did my mind try to "keep
   me safe" today? What would my *on-purpose* self have
   chosen instead?

2. **Archetype Audit:** In this week's toughest moment, which archetype did I use? Which one would have served better? How will I rehearse it?

3. **Certainty Reframe:** Write a letter from your future, certain self to your present self about the project you're pitching. What do they know that you're forgetting?

4. **Emotion as Craft:** Name three emotions your project requires. How will you evoke each one in your meeting/pitch (voice, story, pause, eye contact)?

5. **Five Acknowledgments:** Who will you elevate today with a genuine, specific acknowledgment—and why?

6. **Rejection Debrief:** After a "no," list two skills to practice, one belief to reinforce, and one next bold action within 24 hours.

Micro-Practices (2 minutes each)

- **Magician Switch:** Before meetings, whisper a single word that defines your needed energy (e.g., "Enchant," "Command," "Connect," "Bless"). Step forward as that.

- **Certain Breath:** Inhale 4, hold 4, exhale 6—repeat 4 times while recalling a moment you *were* undeniable. Walk in on that chemistry.

- **Outcome Line:** Write the desired outcome at the top of your notes. If you drift, read it aloud.

CHAPTER 20:
Laughter and Thank You notes with producer Vin Di Bona and writer Erica Gerard

We met at the Italian Television Festival, where human connection did what it always does best: cut through the noise. Erica handed me a thank you note so observant and warm that it stayed with me for days. Vin reminded me why a curated laugh, shared with family, still beats a thousand random scrolls. Together, they're a masterclass in two timeless currencies: gratitude and joy.

Alexia: Erica, how did thank-you notes become your superpower?

Erica: I learned young. In first grade, I wrote President Kennedy during the Cuban Missile Crisis; he wrote back. That letter hung over my bed and taught me that writing could reach anyone—even if I was shy. Later, as a PA at CBS, Connie Chung sent me a note: "Thanks for being a spark in the newsroom." I kept it. I vowed to do the same for others—see them, name them, thank them. Today I type on typewriters (my brand!) and send hundreds of notes a year. Typed letters get opened. More importantly, people feel **seen**.

"A typed letter is a spotlight: it says,
'I see you.'" — Erica

Alexia: Does gratitude still work in a digital world—video thank-you, emails, DMs?
Erica: Use any medium that feels genuine and fits the recipient. If you can't mail it, type it, scan it, and email it. A short selfie video can be lovely if it's personal, not performative. Artists can embed the thank-you in their craft: a musician on sheet music, a child on a paper airplane, an illustrator on a doodle. The point is **signal, not format**.

"Gratitude is a practice;
joy is a service." — Alexia

Alexia: Your three-paragraph formula?
Erica: I call it **Me–You–Us**.

- **Me:** My experience of you/your space (I noticed the Pope photo; your wall of shows).

- **You:** Who I see you to be—your gifts, energy, impact. (This is the little "love letter" inside the letter.)

- **Us:** A bridge to the future—how we might build together or keep in touch.

Alexia: Vin, in the TikTok era, what keeps *America's Funniest Home Videos* special?
Vin: Curation. For each clip that airs, our team combs through piles of submissions to deliver the "best of the best." Viewers are guaranteed a laugh and a family-friendly experience. On social, you hunt and peck; with us, you can sit with your kids, grandparents, and know it's safe, warm, and fun. Internationally, many countries license or co-produce versions, and we trade

clips—it feeds the mothership beautifully.

> *"Me–You–Us: experience, appreciation,*
> *and a bridge to tomorrow." — Erica*

Alexia: What makes a great unscripted concept?
Vin: Surprise and truth. Real reactions, real stakes. Overproducing kills authenticity. Also, every story—from *60 Minutes* to the Housewives—rides on conflict. Find honest tension without faking it.

Alexia: Pitching wisdom for young creators?
Vin: Two things.

1. Bring a **big umbrella**, a clear idea that can last, not just hit once.

   Believe in your show and never take no for an answer.

2. Rehearse. Know your answers. If a network exec calls in the car, pull over, and have your bullet points ready. Persistence + preparation wins.

Alexia: Work–life—do you two ever unplug?
Vin: I join boards where I truly love the subject—cars, museums, alma maters—so service fuels me.
Erica: My morning letters are my gratitude practice. We walk, we take drives, we slow down. A note can be therapy: one sentence of real thanks resets the day.

> *"Curation guarantees the laugh; family-*
> *friendly guarantees you'll share it." — Vin*

Alexia: Culture & heart: the Italian and Jewish threads you bring to life and work?
Vin: Italy taught me visible affection and beauty as a value. I'll

never forget seeing a father and son arm-in-arm—when I came home, I did that with my dad. Years later, the *Cinema Paradiso* theme at the Hollywood Bowl cracked me open; I finally grieved. That film is family to me.

Erica: From Holocaust-survivor roots, I carry remembrance, gratitude, and the duty to connect—one letter at a time.

> *"Bring a big umbrella idea—*
> *and never take no for an answer." — Vin*

Alexia: A full-circle thank-you story?

Vin: A boy found my signed library card in a book from my junior high (decades later!) and wrote to me. He had learning challenges and had been bullied. I invited him to our show taping; it changed something—for him and for me.

Talking with Erica Gerard De Bona and Vin Di Bona reminded me why gratitude and laughter never go out of style. Erica's practice of typed thank-you notes isn't quaint—it's radical. In a noisy, digital world, she proves that being seen is still the greatest gift. Vin shows why a curated laugh, shared across generations, carries more staying power than a thousand swipes.

KEY TAKEAWAYS

Design your medium. Hand-typed, scanned, video, voice note—choose the channel your recipient actually uses.

Pitch for longevity. Can your concept run seasons, travel globally, and sustain a community?

Don't over-produce reality. Protect surprise and truth; the radar audience is sharp.

Prepare like a pro. Rehearse answers, keep bullet points handy, and commit to the call.

Make gratitude a system. 5 minutes daily compound into reputation, rapport, and results

Journaling Questions

1. **Five Faces:** Who meaningfully helped you this month? Draft five Me–You–Us outlines.

2. **Umbrella Test:** How does your current project scale across seasons, countries, and platforms? List three expandable elements.

3. **Authenticity Audit:** Where are you "over-producing" your life or brand? What would the honest version look like?

4. **Grief & Fuel:** What piece of art unlocks emotion for you (*Cinema Paradiso*-style)? How will you honor it in your next pitch or scene?

5. **Conflict Map:** What real tension drives your unscripted (or scripted) idea—and how will you keep it truthful?

CHAPTER 21:
Casting Instincts, and the Long Game with Casting Director Valerie Mc Caffrey

Fridays are for conversations that make you better at your craft. Enter Valerie McCaffrey—121 films cast, former studio exec (Universal, New Line), manager with a sixth sense for talent, and a director whose WWII short *Dirty Bomb* racked up awards and is headed for a feature. She's the definition of multi-hyphenate done right: casting director, talent advocate, and storyteller with receipts.

Alexia: Beauty queen to studio casting? Give us the origin story.
Valerie: I knew at five I'd be in entertainment. My mom was a torch singer who chose family, but she fed my dream—weekend drives down Hollywood Blvd, spotting actors. I acted in school, moved to L.A., and landed at Universal. A boss got fired; two doors opened: production or casting. "You put actors in movies and watch films all day." Sold. Eight years at Universal led to VP Casting at New Line, then independent casting when New Line folded into Warner Bros.

"Studios want longevity; indies need the trigger.
Smart casting serves both."

Alexia: Studio vs. indie—who truly lets you discover unknowns?
Valerie: Both do differently. At Universal, we'd cast unknowns, then tie second/third-picture deals. I pushed that thinking at New Line (after the Jim Carrey "$7M for *The Mask*" lesson).

Studios need marketable names; indies need names to trigger cash. Either way, smart packaging plus real discovery wins.

Alexia: Why add "manager" to your hyphens?
Valerie: I love actors, and I see "it." Example: Madison Thompson—14, unknown. I signed her when no one else did; she went on to *Ozark* and *Grease: Rise of the Pink Ladies*. My job is champion + strategist: roles, timing, material, the long arc. It's cheerleading with rigor.

Alexia: Make the case to hire a casting director (for the indie skeptics).
Valerie: We're market radar. We know who just tested, who's about to pop, who secretly wants your role, and which reps will play ball. We don't just get a "name"—we map the mosaic: bankability, schedule, approvals, and future heat.

"Don't stop the mojo—master one lane, then expand."

Alexia: Diversity: has the pendulum over-swung?
Valerie: It's tougher for some categories now (e.g., white men 50–60), but the field needed widening. As more families encourage kids from underrepresented groups to train and pursue acting, the pipeline evens out. It will be balanced if we keep prioritizing **craft**.

Alexia: What makes a star in the room?
Valerie: Training is sexy. Walk in like they need you (not arrogance—**preparation**). Confidence is born of reps, class, and craft. Looks vary; command doesn't. Think Olympian mindset: daily practice beats "Hollywood vibes."

"Influence doesn't equal attendance. Leads must read."

Alexia: Influencers as leads—helpful or harmful?
Valerie: For bit parts, fine. For leads, they read like everyone else. Follows don't equal tickets. Show me chops.

Alexia: Self-tapes vs. in-room—what changed for you?
Valerie: Self-tapes widen access; more actors can be seen. But callbacks should be in person. On tape, be off-book, neutral background, a solid reader (not scenery-chewing, not wooden). Every glance down is a lost moment.

"Self-tapes widen access; callbacks seal chemistry."

Alexia: Why direct *Dirty Bomb* yourself?
Valerie: Family story. I learned Jewish prisoners sabotaged V-2 rockets—possibly shortening the war. That history grabbed me by the collar. I researched, raised funds, shot in the snow, and at an old detention center. The shorts' success made the mandate clear: expand to a feature.

"Training is sexy. Confidence born of craft fills a room."

Alexia: Three words that define you?
Valerie: Passionate. Stubborn. Hard-working.
Alexia: I'd add relentless and insightful.

Talking with Valerie McCaffrey reminded me why mastery in Hollywood is never one-dimensional. She's lived the studio system, championed unknowns into stars, and now directs stories that matter—proving the hyphen isn't a gimmick but a craft... Her reminder stays with me: longevity isn't luck, its discipline, vision, and the courage to champion voices before the world sees them.

KEY TAKEAWAYS

Prep = Power. Off-book, choices made, body alive—enter like a collaborator.

Package for the long game. Big umbrella ideas + rising talent + strategic deals.

Use the pipeline. Casting directors are intel hubs—bankability, timing, and taste.

Influencer math ≠ performance. Social reach is a bonus, never a substitute.

Make a film because you must. If the story grips your soul, that's your green light.

Journaling Questions

1. **Olympian Audit:** What reps/classes are you committing to weekly for 90 days? Track them.

2. **Room Energy:** Write the three adjectives you want casting to feel in your presence. How will you embody them?

3. **Pipeline Map:** List five casting directors whose taste fits your work. How will you get on their radar (festival shorts, tapes, showcases)?

4. **Self-Tape Reset:** Which two technical mistakes do you repeat? What's your fix (reader, backdrop, lighting, eyeline)?

5. **Story Mandate:** What story won't let you go—and what's the first non-negotiable step this month?

Micro-Practices (2 minutes each)

- **Beat the Page:** Mark beats on sides, then run it once eyes-up—no glances down.

- **Director's Logline:** State your character's need in one breath before every take.

- **Casting Kudo:** Send one specific acknowledgment a week to a CD/rep after a session—zero asks.

CHAPTER 22:
Rewriting Who Leads in Nature Docs with Wildlife Producer Vanessa Berlowitz

National Geographic's *Queens* took four years, traveled continents, and flipped the lens: female-led animal societies told by a women-forward crew. Executive producer and Wildstar Films cofounder Vanessa Berlowitz (ex-BBC Natural History Unit) proves you can deliver breath-stealing spectacle and move the industry forward at the same time—training new voices behind the camera while honoring the matriarchs in front of it.

Alexia: Climate change showed up while you filmed. What did you see?

Vanessa: A once-in-20-year East African drought—right in the middle of production. Our director, Faith Musembi, had been following elephants, including a blind matriarch, Selenge. After a COVID pause, she returned to devastation; Selenge hadn't survived. We all know the data, but witnessing loss at that scale turned statistics into stakes.

"We turned statistics into stakes
—drought isn't a headline when your matriarch doesn't return."

Alexia: You centered women on both sides of the camera—why and how?

Vanessa: If we're telling stories of female leadership in nature, we should also change who tells them. We recruited two of the world's few female DPs—Justine Evans and Sophie Darlington—to lead and mentor. With support from camera partners, we trained emerging women from Brazil, Alaska, Kenya, Tanzania, and beyond—reviewing rushes, loaning pro gear, and promoting them into key roles. The production became a living academy, not a quota.

"We didn't hire women for optics;
we built a pipeline."

Alexia: Where did the series idea come from?

Vanessa: Years following elephant matriarchs for *Dynasties* seeded a bigger question: What if we focused on female power across species? I pitched Nat Geo's Janet Han Vissering a 1-off (lion vs. hyena matriarchs in Ngorongoro). She said, "That's a series." We mapped six habitats and leadership styles—and discovered even more female-led systems than the textbooks list.

"Leadership in nature is plural
—memory, muscle, consensus, sisterhood."

Alexia: The bonobo episode hit hard.

Vanessa: In DRC, orphaned bonobos would literally die of heartbreak without constant comfort. At the Mama Bonobo Sanctuary, local women—many themselves survivors of conflict—become 24/7 foster "mothers," rebuilding trust before rewilding youngsters into forest enclosures. It's mutual healing: women and bonobos recovering together.

"Local voices aren't a luxury;
they're the truth."

Alexia: Why Angela Bassett?
Vanessa: She is the queen. Range for drama and humor, gravitas, and a lived commitment to empowering underrepresented voices—aligned with our training mission. She came on after watching a cut, then leaned in as executive producer to amplify the series.

"Angela didn't just narrate; she championed the mission."

Alexia: If people want to help—but can't go to Africa—what's useful?
Vanessa: Two lanes. For filmmakers: we need **local voices**—tell the stories where you live, use bold craft (humor, drama, pop culture) to compete for attention. For everyone: support field orgs you discover in the series (e.g., sanctuaries, anti-poaching units), volunteer if you can, and—crucially—**vote for environmental policy**.

Alexia: What can humans learn from "queens"?
Vanessa: Leadership has many shapes. Elephants lead with memory and calm; hyenas with unapologetic force; bonobos with consensus and care; lionesses with ride-or-die sisterhood. I loved watching an elder elephant freeze at a new road—and defer to a younger female to cross. That's modern leadership, too: experience plus adaptive humility.

Talking with Vanessa Berlowitz reminded me that who tells the story is as important as the story itself. With Queens, she redefined nature documentaries—spotlighting female-led animal societies while training a new generation of women behind the lens. Her work makes the stakes visceral: drought isn't just data when you watch a blind elephant matriarch vanish, and healing isn't abstract when women and bonobos recover side by side. What stays with me is her vision of leadership—whether in elephants, hyenas, or humans—as memory, force, care, and sisterhood woven together.

KEY TAKEAWAYS

Train while you shoot. Convert long productions into rolling academies with paid ladders up.

Tell, don't preach. Lead with story and character; let care follow connection.

Map leadership styles. Build ensembles with contrasting "powers" (memory, force, consensus, loyalty).

Center proximity. Collaborate with people who live with the wildlife—co-own the POV.

Make help actionable. Point audiences to orgs, volunteer paths, and policy levers.

Journaling Questions

1. **Your Matriarch Map:** Which leadership style do you default to (memory/force/consensus/sisterhood)? What situation asks for a different one?

2. **Local Lens:** What nonhuman neighbors (urban foxes, pigeons, tidepools) hold a story only you can tell? Draft a 2-minute pitch.

3. **Preach-less Rewrite:** Take one "issue" scene and recast it entirely through character stakes and surprise.

Micro-Practices (2 minutes each)

- **Cut to Character:** Replace one statistic in your script with a named individual (animal or human) and a verb.

- **Mentor Ping:** Send a specific note offering review of a reel/rushes for an emerging filmmaker.

- **Policy Check:** Look up one current environmental vote in your area; note your representative's stance.

CHAPTER 23:
Stronger through Faith
with actress Eva La Rue

Emmy-winning actor (and multi-hyphenate) Ava LaRue has moved between daytime icons (*All My Children*, *The Young and the Restless*), primetime (*CSI: Miami*), faith-forward projects (*Finding Love in Quarantine*), and three seasons hosting *Chicken Soup for the Soul: Animal Tales*. She's equal parts artist, activist, and optimist—Baha'i values, animal rescue receipts, and a no-Plan-B career philosophy that feels like a masterclass in staying power.

> *"The 'no' often comes from someone unqualified to say yes."*

Alexia: You grew up with very little. How did you choose an unstable career without a safety net?
Ava: There *was* no net. That lit the fire—but not as fear. It never occurred to me that I wouldn't succeed. Plan B wasn't in my vocabulary. The family needed money; performing was the passion. I went all-in on Plan A.

Alexia: Early training or straight to work?
Ava: Straight in. Child commercials, teen musical theater, dinner theater—then full-time after high school. I would've majored in theater anyway. The school of life paid and taught at once.

> *"Plan B wasn't in my vocabulary. Plan A was the plan."*

Alexia: Your faith?

Ava: I'm Baha'i. After my brother died when I was 11, my mom searched for spiritual ground and found it. What resonated: one God, one humanity, many prophets equal. And the Baha'i emphasis on **independent investigation of truth**. You aren't "in" until you choose at 15. That openness still guides me.

"Independent investigation of truth—that's my compass."

Alexia: Animals and advocacy have been constant.

Ava: Always. I grew up riding horses bareback in a rural town, and later, dressage and jumpers. I hosted *Animal Tales*—stories where animals save people and people save animals. Interdependence is real. And yes, I'm thrilled Santorini's phasing out donkey rides—welfare matters.

Alexia: "Charity should always be a constant"—your quote. What does giving do for *you*?

Ava: When life crushes you—and it does—showing up for others pulls you out. Not performative red carpets; *present service*. It's reciprocal: you acknowledge courage, not pity, circumstance, and somehow the energy stitches you back together.

"Service isn't optics; it's presence."

Alexia: Latina in Hollywood—progress or tokenism?

Ava: Better than a decade ago, but we're not there. Too few Latinas lead series; too many still in the "maid/hooker/drug addict" box. *All My Children* was cutting-edge with the Santos family; *CSI: Miami* put two Latines in the core cast. More, please—and not just as the fourth lead.

Alexia: Career rule for newcomers?

Ava: You must be **single-minded**. If you can "try" it, it's not for you. The rejection will flatten you unless the love is bigger. Don't hand your worth to an opinion. Often "no" comes from someone unqualified to say "yes."

"If you can 'try' acting, it's not for you."

Alexia: What's next?

Ava: *Pine Valley*—a nighttime reimagining of *All My Children*. Pilot first; huge built-in fan base. Fingers crossed.

Talking with Ava LaRue reminded me why longevity in Hollywood isn't about luck, it's about conviction. She never had a Plan B, only the fire of Plan A, and that single-mindedness carried her from daytime icons to primetime hits, from hosting to activism. What grounds her isn't just craft but compass: Baha'i values, service as presence, and a fierce love for animals and advocacy. Ava insists rejection can't define you, because most "no's" come from those unqualified to say "yes."

KEY TAKEAWAYS

Belief + craft. Positive mindset isn't fluff; it fuels the stamina to train, audition, and repeat.

Values are strategy. A clear worldview (Ava's Baha'i lens) simplifies choices under pressure.

Service regulates. When you're spiraling, help someone. It reorients identity from "performer" to "person."

Representation must be central, not decorative. Push for Latine leads in the first three slots, not as an "also."

Guard your inputs. Early on, don't read about yourself. Protect the creative psyche.

Journaling Questions

1. **Plan A Audit:** If you eliminated your Plan B today, what three actions would change this week?

2. **Gatekeeper Reframe:** Recall your last "no." Was it about your value—or their bandwidth/brand? What's your next door?

3. **Service Reset:** List two skills you can donate this month (reading to camera, grant proofreading, shelter volunteering). Pick one and schedule it.

4. **Voice & Values:** Write your one-paragraph "independent investigation of truth." How does it guide career decisions?

Micro-Practices (2 minutes each)

- **Inbox Courage:** Send one ask you've been avoiding (rep, casting, mentor coffee).

- **Credit Swap:** Replace "I wasn't chosen" with "I'm building reps; next rep tomorrow."

- **Unfollow/Refill:** Mute three accounts that trigger imposter syndrome; follow three that teach craft.

- **Animal Kindness:** Donate or signal-boost a local rescue; add a monthly $5 auto pledge.

CHAPTER 24:
The CEO of You, Inc with Stage 32 Founder RB Botto

I've known RB Botto since the earliest days of **Stage 32**, where I was honored to be invited as one of the very first educators. I taught classes on **pitching before festivals and markets** and on **how to network with global decision makers** — the same lessons I'd spent years practicing in Hollywood and beyond.

Through Stage 32, I also discovered extraordinary creatives, including **Sandi Jerome**, who today co-writes this very book with me. That's the ripple effect of RB's vision: he built not just a platform, but a movement that connects people across the globe.

So when I sat down with RB, it wasn't just another interview. It was a reunion between two kindred spirits who believe that creativity, community, and mindset can change the world.

"People's lives are a direct reflection of the expectations of their peer group." — Tony Robbins

"If you're a creative, you're already the CEO of you, inc."

Alexia: What sparked the idea for Stage 32?
RB: I needed it. As an actor, writer, and producer, I wanted community, positivity, and direct access beyond gatekeepers. The industry is tribal — so I built the tribe I couldn't find.

Alexia: Was it hard to balance your platform with your own creative career?
RB: Yes, at first. But relationships are the fuel of this business. Everything I've accomplished in the last 10 years has come from Stage 32. Networking isn't optional — it's survival.

Alexia: Let's talk personal branding. How did "RB" become more than just a nickname?
RB: Your personal brand *is* your currency. I became RB — not Richard — because that's who people connected with. If you're a creative, you're already an entrepreneur. You're the CEO of *You, Inc.* The question is: how do you want your company to be perceived?

Alexia: What about rejection and the dark times?
RB: Experience changes your lens. Rejection no longer spirals me — it fuels me. And the antidote to dark times? Surround yourself with positive voices. Curate your circle, cut out the negative. Control what you can control.

Alexia: What advice would you give to creatives still trying to "break in"?
RB: Stop waiting for permission. Build your own momentum. Celebrate other people's success because there's room for everyone — and when you help lift others up, your opportunities multiply.

"Celebrate other people's success
— there's room for everyone."

*RB has always reminded us: "Celebrate other people's success — there's room for everyone." That's why Stage 32 became not just a platform, but a global **movement**.*

I've seen it firsthand, as an educator on Stage 32 since day one, as a connector discovering creatives like Sandi Jerome, and as a producer navigating a global industry. RB built a stage for the world, and in doing so, he taught all of us that our greatest asset isn't just our talent, it's our brand, our resilience, and our willingness to lift others as we rise.

KEY TAKEAWAYS

You are a brand – Every creative is an entrepreneur: you are the CEO of You, Inc. How you show up, what you stand for, and how people experience you is your currency. Authenticity matters— RB became "RB" because that's who people resonated with.
Curate your circle – Rejection and dark times are inevitable. Protect your energy by surrounding yourself with positive voices, cutting negativity, and focusing on what you can control. Experience turns setbacks into fuel.
Lift as you rise – Success multiplies when you celebrate others. Helping others succeed doesn't diminish your opportunities; it expands them. Collaboration, generosity, and recognition are as powerful as talent itself.
Momentum over permission – Waiting for permission is a trap. Build your own opportunities, take action, and own your path.

Journaling Questions
1. Where do you feel isolated or lacking community? How could you build your own tribe?
2. How would you define your personal brand? Does it align with the person people actually connect with?

3. Who in your circle fuels you, and who drains you? How can you curate your relationships for growth?
4. When have you celebrated someone else's success recently? How did it impact you?
5. Where are you waiting for permission instead of creating momentum?

Practical Tips

- **Tribe-building exercise:** Identify three people, groups, or communities you want to connect with and take one concrete step this week to engage.
- **Brand audit:** Write down how you currently present yourself vs. how you want to be perceived. Adjust one thing to align your presence with your goals.
- **Energy check:** Make a list of five people who energize you and five who drain you. Plan how to spend more time with the former and set boundaries with the latter.
- **Celebrate others:** Reach out to one person this week to genuinely acknowledge their success—watch how that energy returns.
- **Momentum action:** Pick one idea or project you've been waiting for to launch. Take the first step, however small, without asking permission.

CHAPTER 25:
Ten Pages a Day with writer Sandi Jerome

It's said that success leaves clues. In Sandi Jerome's case, the clue is consistency—she writes ten pages a day, every day. That discipline alone could fill volumes, but when paired with her curiosity, research skills, and sheer creative drive, it becomes unstoppable.

There is a part 2 to this book, authored by my client, Sandi Jerome. I wanted to have her perspective and journey so that readers can also hear it from those who have a soul's calling to become a creative in Hollywood. Sandi has soaked up like a sponge information and guidance, not just from myself, but she is also a staggeringly accurate researcher and executor of everything thrown her way. She does it all with the wonder and joy of a child, which is why we came together to write this book.

It was RB Botto's Stage32 where I met one of my clients, Sandi Jerome. She had pitched her spec thriller/horror script, LAST WOMAN, and I asked to read it—and loved her enthusiasm. In the first year after signing a contract on March 15, 2024, she has written five "writer for hire" scripts:

- HIJACKED – book adaptation to script

- AUGIE – original sequel screenplay, director attached, being produced by Little Studio Films.

- LAST POE – original horror screenplay written with Disney artist Guy Vasilovich.

- JAKE AND CLARA – book adaptation, David Stokes (author of CAMELOT'S COUSIN, optioned by Blair Underwood).

- DID LOVE JUST HIT ME — original screenplay being produced by Little Studio Films.

These were all done for a lower deferred payment and a clause that if the budget exceeds $10 million, they follow WGA minimums, which means over $600,000 in income for her if the films get produced. Not bad for our first year together.

As you'll read in the next section written by Sandi, "writing is life" for her. She writes at least ten pages a day, every day. In addition to the above "work for hire," she wrote three spec screenplays— CHRISTMAS CALLING, EMMA AND THE CHOCOLATE FACTORY (formerly CHRISTMAS BONBONS), and PYTHON PURSUIT (a horror movie she co-wrote with our editor, Heidi Stangeland, after listening to one of my podcasts about the illegal pet trade). That script now has directors attached and is getting serious attention.

Sandi also writes books. While researching AUGIE (the sequel to MAMA DALLAS), she joked she had so much information about Jody's Italian family that she could write a book. I encouraged her to do it to protect the IP of the franchise. She did, and wrote MAMA DALLAS AND AUGIE, which was published by my new company, Little Studios Publishing. Sandi merged her publishing business, Smiling Eagle, into mine and became an associate publisher.

Her range is remarkable. She followed that with CHURCHILL'S MUM — THE STORY OF JENNIE JEROME — AN AMERICAN HEIRESS, written with author and Churchill expert David R. Stokes. And she's already developing it into a limited series.

As a screenwriter, Sandi was originally a feature writer, having graduated from UCLA's advanced screenwriting program, but she expanded into television after winning the Native American Media Alliance Fellowship. There, she learned TV writing from AFI instructors and a working TV writer mentor. Since then, she's developed multiple TV bibles, from the teen detective WILMA WALLABY series to TECHNICALLY SOCCER, a Ted Lasso-style comedy with international appeal.

In her "spare" time, she polished her spec scripts, built new websites, and created marketing assets for herself and for Little Studio Publishing. How does she do all this? Because Sandi is a professional. In her previous career as the owner of a technology company, she never stopped thinking of herself as a writer. Even on planes, flying 200,000 miles a year, she wrote.

With my help as her manager, she's now combining artistry with a career that is both creatively fulfilling and financially promising. And while I don't pick favorite among my clients, Sandi is high on my list. I'm proud to introduce the next section of my book, written by one of my favorite writers, Sandi Jerome, who proves, one ten-page day at a time, that persistence is the true currency of Hollywood dreams.

PART TWO
SANDI JEROME

CHAPTER 1
An origin story

Why Am I Doing This?

There are thousands of books about how to write screenplays. Most will tell you where to put your slug lines, how to format dialogue, or what a "beat" really means. This is not one of those books.

Instead, this is about the WHY. Because let's be honest: after getting bad coverage or another rejection email, you might find yourself thinking:

"Why am I a screenwriter?
Why do I make myself so miserable?"

I've asked myself that too. The answer always comes back to this: because I'm a storyteller.

The Heart of Storytelling

When directors or actors win awards, it's easy to forget that they're standing on the shoulders of writers. We build the foundation. We create the worlds. We know what happens next before anyone else does.

When I write, I disappear. Two weeks vanish into a creative fog where I live inside my characters. If they're walking the streets of Detroit, then in my imagination, so am I. It's a kind of "method writing" — I fully embody them.

And no, AI can't do this. (It might help format your outline faster, but it's never going to walk around Detroit in your head the way a writer can.)

Wrangling Cats

If you've read Part One, you've seen how many journeys converge in this business—actors, directors, producers. As a writer, your job is to hand them the story that unites all of their chaos.

Director Jay Russell said it best on Alexia's podcast: *"directing to a great degree is like wrangling cats—because the cats run off in all different directions, you've got to get them somehow in the same room together."*

Screenwriting is like that, too. Ideas, characters, dialogue, they all scatter in your brain like a herd of caffeinated cats. Your job is to herd them into the same story.

Overcoming Doubt (and Ageism)

I've been writing for years, but only recently embraced it as my primary career. When I complained to a colleague that Coverfly only shows recent contest wins, he didn't sugarcoat it: *"that's probably because they think it's time for you to step aside and let someone younger move forward."*

Ouch. That one stung.

But then Dimitris Logothetis gave me the perspective I needed: *"Why not you? Nobody's better. Nobody's smarter. Nobody has more right to succeed than you—because of your determination."*

And Betsy Sullenger reminded me of the importance of joy: *"Now that I'm older, I am by God going to experience the full measure of joy in what I do. And I'm going to hire department heads who are joyful and like-minded."*

I've adopted that mindset. I avoid negative people. I wake up happy to write.

And Ariana Savalas? She gave me my favorite mantra: *"The biggest comfort my father gave me was this—it's never too late. Ever, ever, ever. My dad became a sex symbol at 50."*

So no, I'm not "too old." I'm not "too late." And neither are you.

The Day I Became a Screenwriter

I can pinpoint the exact day over twenty years ago when I decided to become a screenwriter.

I was in a Portland law office, helping a client patent his "million-dollar idea." (Spoiler: I didn't make a million.) His app, "One in the Music," was supposed to match people by musical taste. Flowers? Too old-fashioned. His version of romance was sending each other songs.

It wasn't a paying gig. I got stock in exchange for writing his algorithm. Since I'm writing this book at my desk instead of on my yacht, you can guess how that turned out.

At lunch, I ended up in the breakroom with the son of one of the attorneys. He was reading TWILIGHT. The kid gave me the best pitch I'd ever heard—so good I left work that day and went straight to Barnes & Noble to buy Stephenie Meyer's book.

That night, lightning struck: *what if we could back up our minds like computers?* I imagined a villain, dying, who backs up his mind and uploads it into a bright young kid. It was a great MOVIE idea.

The next evening, I dashed back to Barnes & Noble, straight to the screenwriting section. I grabbed Cynthia Whitcomb's THE WRITER'S GUIDE TO WRITING YOUR SCREENPLAY. Flipping through it was another revelation:

Screenplays looked like code. Instead of telling a computer what to do, they told a director, a set designer, and an actor what to do. A screenplay was a program for a movie. I was a programmer. I could be a screenwriter.

"A screenplay is a program for a movie."

The Odds (and Why They Don't Matter)

Then came the gut punch. On the back of Cynthia's book was a list of screenplays she had written and sold. The shock? How many were never produced!

Think about it. The WGA has about 25,000 members. Over 50,000 scripts get registered every year. My guess? 100,000 active screenwriters are competing for a limited number of slots.

But here's the good news: last year, hundreds of new films and series were produced. Compare that to NASA's astronaut program: 12,000 apply, 10 are accepted. Your odds in Hollywood are better.

And besides, I didn't let odds stop me from building and selling a tech company. Why let them stop me here?

Failure, to me, is only when you quit. Everything else is practice.

My So-Called "Overnight" Success

Fast forward twenty years.

My manager, Alexia, signed me in 2024 under Little Studio Films' management. In my first year, I wrote and sold five screenplays on deferred payment deals. If the budget exceeds $10 million, I'll make over $600,000. Not bad for a "non-WGA newbie."

But here's the truth: I've only collected $2,500 so far. That's the reality of deferred deals. If you're in this business for fast money, you'll be sorely disappointed.
I'm not an overnight success. I'm a twenty-year overnight success.

Do You Have the Right Stuff? (HIJACKED)

Richard Bach said: *"A professional writer is a writer who doesn't give up."*

That became my North Star. My proof of having the "right stuff" came with HIJACKED.

Getting Ahead of Myself

Here's my secret weapon: I get ahead of myself. I pack a week early for trips. I lay out tomorrow's clothes before I go to bed. And yes, I write treatments for projects no one's asked me to write.

That's how HIJACKED happened.

Alexia casually mentioned a producer chasing the rights to a book about a FedEx plane hijacking. That night, I found the book, read it, and drafted a treatment. The next morning, I sent it to Alexia.

She hadn't asked for it. She probably thought I was nuts. But she forwarded it anyway.

That's what landed me the meeting.

Faith, Race, and Story Integrity

Some producers had avoided the project because the hijacker was Black, and the pilots were white. Post–Rodney King, it felt like a minefield.

But to me, it wasn't about race. It was about workplace violence, greed, faith, and unimaginable heroism.

That clarity made the story viable again.

Producers, Producers, Producers

And here's the lesson: once the script was written, the real marathon began. Coverage, rewrites, notes. Producers came on board.

Suddenly, more producers joined. That's how films get made. Scripts don't move alone. They collect producers like barnacles until one of them has the clout (or luck) to push it across the finish line.

And My First Idea?

And what about BACKUP, the idea that started it all? Twenty years later, no producer has read it. Not one.

But that's okay. Because the point isn't one script. The point is persistence. The point is to write the next one.

Closing

Writing isn't my "third act." It's not a hobby. It's my life. I wake up excited to write. I fail a lot. I get rejected constantly. And I keep going.
If you're still here, still reading, still dreaming, then maybe writing is your life too.
So the only question left is: Do you have the right stuff?

CHAPTER 2
The trifecta of tools, skills, and practice

Education – Do You Need It?

"You wasted $150,000 on an education you could have got for $1.50 in late fees at the public library."
—Matt Damon in GOOD WILL HUNTING

The Accidental Student

I wasn't born with raw talent for ANYTHING. I was shy. I stuttered. I could trip over a bobby pin in a shag carpet. My mom used to joke that coordination skipped me entirely. And yet, through sheer stubbornness, I became a public speaker, shared a stage (and a lounge!) with First Lady Barbara Bush, and even became certified as a yoga instructor.

That's my story in a nutshell: afraid of everything, but willing to throw myself at it until I figure it out.

So, of course, I threw myself into education too. I started in International Agriculture because my original plan was to teach the world how to grow food. From there, I veered into Agribusiness, then Business, then Accounting and Computer Science. And eventually, somehow, screenwriting.

This chapter isn't about my zigzag career path. It's about education and whether it matters if you want to be a screenwriter.

Degrees, Film Schools, and the Big Question

Do you need an MFA? An English degree? Film school? For TV writing, school can be valuable for contacts, professors who know showrunners, workshops that simulate writers' rooms, and classmates who become collaborators. For features, I'm not convinced it matters.

If you have raw talent and a great idea, you can do what I did: buy a book, download some screenwriting software, and just start. My first was Cynthia Whitcomb's THE WRITER'S GUIDE TO WRITING YOUR SCREENPLAY. I've probably bought a dozen since. My favorite now? Alexia Melocchi's AN INSIDER'S SECRET: MASTERING THE HOLLYWOOD PATH. That book convinced me I needed representation—and here we are.

But back to school. Even though I was already a CPA and computer consultant making $3,500–$5,000 a day back in the early 2000s, I wanted to learn screenwriting properly. So, I went to UCLA.

UCLA, USC, AFI, and the Heavy Hitters

UCLA's online screenwriting program was my path in. My instructors? Jack Sowards (STAR TREK II: THE WRATH OF KHAN) and Jim Schmerer (MACGYVER, CHIPS, FANTASY ISLAND). They told me—and my classmate Dana Biscotti Myskowski—that we were the best in the class. That encouragement lit my fire. UCLA grads include Francis Ford Coppola, Alexander Payne

(SIDEWAYS), and David Koepp (JURASSIC PARK). Not bad company.

Of course, some argue USC's School of Cinematic Arts is the gold standard. Alumni include George Lucas, Shonda Rhimes, and John Singleton. Their program is as much about industry connections as craft.

When I won the Native American Media Alliance Fellowship, my mentor Matt Black (UMMA with Sandra Oh) was also on faculty at AFI. AFI is smaller, more intimate, and mentor-driven, with alumni like David Lynch, Darren Aronofsky, and Sam Esmail (MR. ROBOT). Matt loved Lynch so much that he tattooed an ear on his arm from BLUE VELVET. (Confession: I hated BLUE VELVET.)

NYU Tisch? Dramatic writing royalty: Kenneth Lonergan (MANCHESTER BY THE SEA), Tony Kushner (ANGELS IN AMERICA), Donald Glover. Columbia? Kathryn Bigelow (THE HURT LOCKER), James Mangold (LOGAN), Simon Kinberg (X-MEN).

But here's the kicker: one of my two favorite writers, Aaron Sorkin, wasn't a screenwriting major at all. He studied theater acting at Syracuse. Raw talent dripped from his pen. And my FAVORITE TV writer ever, Chuck Lorre (THE BIG BANG THEORY, TWO AND A HALF MEN, YOUNG SHELDON), dropped out of SUNY to write songs—including the TEENAGE MUTANT NINJA TURTLES theme song. He never went back to school, but he did get an honorary degree. I like to imagine he paid his overdue library fines first.

So... Do You Need It?

Here's my take:

- **No, you don't need it.** Many greats never set foot in a film school.

- **Yes, it can help.** If you're young, it gives you contact and confidence. If you're like me— "a quart low on raw talent"—education can help you acquire skills.

If you've got time and money, go for it. UCLA, USC, AFI, NYU, Columbia—take your pick. If not? Buy a couple of books, read scripts, download Final Draft (or the free FadeIn). Write.

Just don't waste years on an MFA in "Creative Writing" thinking Shakespeare sonnets will make you a screenwriter. Screenwriting is about people, action, and dialogue—not Elizabethan poetry.

Matt Damon and Ben Affleck proved the point with GOOD WILL HUNTING. They won the Oscar without an MFA. Damon's line in the film still rings true: education can be the best investment—or the biggest waste of money.

The education you need depends less on
tuition and more on determination.

Finding the Time to Write

Regardless of degrees, this is the real education: showing up every day.
I write 10 pages a day, every day. That's 20+ screenplays, multiple pilots, and a stack of books. My secret? I get up at 4 a.m. Four a.m. until noon is sacred. It's quiet, its mine, and it's

productive. Back when I ran my software company, I used those hours to code. Now I use them to write.

Traveling 200,000 miles a year as a consultant? I wrote in airports, on planes, in hotels. Today, I write on a treadmill desk. While logging my daily 5K, I also log new pages.
Writing is my job, my hobby, and my exercise.

My Nemesis: Zoom Meetings

What I don't love? Zoom.
Zooms are a productivity black hole for writers. You can't write while you're waiting for someone who may or may not show up. Notes get muddled. Producers forget what they said last time.

I once asked if I could change the main character, delete characters, and alter the storyline. "Yes, you have complete control," they said. I submitted Act One—and they came back saying, "No, keep everything the same."
That's the reality. Until you're Shonda Rhimes (who famously stopped taking notes on SCANDAL after Season 1), you bend. You rewrite. You compromise.

My advice: after every meeting, send an email summarizing the notes. That way, when someone forgets what they asked for, you have proof.

Getting Started

People often tell me they have "an idea for a movie." My response? WRITE IT DOWN.
I keep notebooks everywhere. I email myself ideas. I even dictate to Siri. But here's the thing: ideas aren't scripts. If you're serious,

read actual screenplays. Writing in that format isn't natural—it's learned.

And yes, invest in software. Screenplays have a rigid format for a reason. If you're fighting Word documents, you'll quit before you start.

Screenwriting Software: The Tools of the Trade

I've used them all: Movie Magic Screenwriter, Final Draft, FadeIn. Here's the short version:

- **Final Draft**: Industry heavyweight. 95% of Hollywood uses it. Expensive, clunky, but standard. If you want to collaborate, you'll end up here.

- **FadeIn**: Sleek, cheap, powerful. My favorite for clean writing. Exporting to Final Draft isn't perfect, though.

- **Movie Magic Screenwriter**: Old-school. Great templates, especially for plays and novels. Less intuitive, but still useful.

Others worth noting: WriterDuet (real-time collaboration), Celtx (indie favorite with production tools), StudioBinder (comprehensive but overkill for some), Highland (minimalist, created by John August).

In the end, the tool doesn't matter. The story does. But the wrong tool can slow you down. So, pick one that gets out of your way.

Closing Thought

When I ran my tech company, I worked 14-hour days, coding payroll software, meeting investors, and running a team. Compared to that, writing feels easy—because I have the tools, the discipline, and the love for it.

Do you need education? Maybe. Maybe not. What you definitely need is grit, time, and persistence.

Because in screenwriting, as in life, talent is only the beginning.

CHAPTER 3
The Business Of Show Business (and lessons learned)

Find a Structure

If I could go back twenty years, I would have learned STRUCTURE better.

At UCLA, they drilled into me the classic 3-Act structure—set-up, confrontation, resolution. It's the skeleton of almost every Hollywood movie. But what I didn't realize back then is that there are many more ways to build a story.

Hallmark, for example, uses a 9-Act structure. During my Native American Media Alliance Fellowship, my AFI instructor taught us the 8-sequence structure. And today, for most scripts, my go-to is **Save the Cat**, Blake Snyder's beat sheet that so many writers (including my manager, Alexia) swear by.

If you have Final Draft, you can cheat. Just click "New from Template," then "Structure," and select Blake Snyder's Save the Cat. For horror, though, I prefer the 8-sequence structure—so I switch to "Act and Sequence" in Final Draft.

The truth is that every genre has its own flavor of structure. And once you know the rules, your job is to twist them.

Evan Daugherty said it best: *"There absolutely is a formula, but the creative challenge lies in how do you take something that is a formula and make it feel fresh and restructure it in a surprising way."*

And as Hallmark executive Jon Eskenas explained about their 9-Act TV movies: *"Usually, there are nine acts in a hallmark movie, eight commercial breaks. The first act is about 20 minutes, the rest are seven to ten minutes, with your fourth act landing at the one-hour mark."*

It took me forever to get that structure right. Finally, I gave up and did what any former programmer would do: I wrote a **Claude AI program** to track Hallmark beats and make sure my script stayed on path. Yes, I literally programmed my own structure checker.

Write a Variety of Scripts

Every business need inventory. For writers, that inventory is called a **spec script**—your samples, your calling cards.

Back when I owned my software company, we called it a beta demo. You had to show investors something tangible. Screenwriting is the same. You can't walk into a meeting with one lonely script and expect to sell yourself as a writer.

I have thrillers, horror, fantasy, family drama, comedy, sci-fi, rom-com, Hallmark Christmas scripts, and multiple TV pilots. Some I wrote in hotel rooms and on airplanes while working 14-hour days as a consultant. A few placed in the Nicholl Fellowships or Austin Film Festival, but most were far from "perfect."

Only after I sold my company and could write full-time did I begin cranking out what I'd call "professional" specs. Diversity fellowships helped too—I won the Native American Media

Alliance Fellowship, which taught me how to write for TV and helped me transform a few of my features into pilots.

Don't pigeonhole yourself. Write across genres.
Your script inventory is your store window.

Coverage and Feedback

Here's the painful truth: your "perfect" script probably isn't perfect. What you likely need is one (or all) of three things:

1. Better plot structure

2. Stronger character development

3. Snappier dialogue

The only way to find out? Feedback.
I've had readers who focused only on FORMAT—and honestly, those comments drive me crazy. One guy flagged almost every slug line in my script. I was taught to write:

EXT. CHICAGO, SUBURBS, HOUSE, KITCHEN – DAY

Now the trend is:

EXT. CHICAGO – SUBURBS – HOUSE – KITCHEN – DAY

Does it really matter? Probably not. But nitpicky readers will die on that hill.

My advice: read every article you can about screenplay format and make yourself a personal checklist. Mine includes searching for double spaces after periods (a leftover habit from typing class) and changing double dashes to single. It's tedious, but it saves you from giving a bored reader ammunition.

But the GOOD feedback—the kind that stings at first but makes you better—comes from people like Alexia's client and fellow writer/editor, Heidi. Heidi once told me, "YOUR CHARACTERS DON'T ALL SOUND LIKE THEMSELVES. THEY NEED UNIQUE VOICES."

She gave me specific line edits, and she was right. Now, I test dialogue by stripping character names and reading the scene aloud. If I can't tell who's speaking by voice alone, the writing isn't strong enough.
I trust Heidi so much now that I hire her for all my coverage, and we even co-write thrillers and horror together.

Learn to love tough notes. They hurt, but they're how you grow.

Contests: Enter or Not?

I'm a contest junkie. I admit it.
And it hasn't been a total waste. I've had scripts in the top 3% on Coverfly, several on the Red List, and five in the top 20%. Two of my scripts, LAST HAND and FIRST MAN, reached Nicholl quarterfinals out of 6,000 entries.

Early on, I loved contests because they gave me validation—and coverage. Yes, you'll get rejected. Yes, it will sting. But the notes you get from contest readers are often the same you'd hear from readers at agencies and production companies. Learning to survive that criticism is part of your education.

Jonathan Silverman said it best: *"Make sure you love what you're doing. Because there will be joys and successes but also pain and failures. As long as you love it, that's what matters."*

The Upside of Contests

- **Exposure & Recognition**: Finalists often get read by producers and execs.

- **Networking**: Many contests host events where you can meet peers and mentors. I once won a pitch contest for a reality show (WINNERS), which got me meetings on the Warner Bros. lot. I wasn't prepared (rookie mistake), but the opportunity was real.

- **Cash Prizes**: After twenty years of entering, I finally won $200 with a YOUNG SHELDON spec! (It covered maybe two days of groceries, but still—it felt great.)

- **Validation**: A placement can give you the confidence to keep going.

The Downside of Contests

- **Negativity**: I once met a contest reader who admitted he recycled old notes when he was tired. Imagine paying $50 to have someone skim your script and cut-and-paste feedback.

- **Subjectivity**: It's a beauty pageant. Some readers love horror, some hate it. Some are in a bad mood. It's luck of the draw.

- **Costs**: Entry fees add up fast. It's like gambling—lots of coins, few jackpots.

Limited Payoff: Even winning doesn't guarantee representation or sales. You still have to hustle.

As Alexia says, *"Don't ever read coverage from someone who isn't willing to put their name on it."*

Use contests as training wheels, not your entire career strategy.

AI and Coverage

Like it or not, AI is creeping into script coverage. Studios are already using services like Callaia, which analyzes story, characters, comps, and even potential cast. Others like Prescene, Scriptreader.AI, and RivetAI promise to slash coverage times. I even built my own Claude program to test my Hallmark scripts against 9-Act beats.

Will contests start using AI to judge? Probably. And like the internet once was, it's not going away. Don't fight it, learn how to make it work for you.

Fierce Competition

Here's the scale of what you're up against:

- **Page International 2025**: 9,115 entries.

- **Austin Film Festival 2024**: 10,500 submissions.

Your odds? Slim. That's why I now focus on smaller, niche contests like Stage32, which are specific to genre.
Oh, and about my 2025 resolution in all caps: NO MORE CONTESTS. Yeah, we'll see.

Final Word on Structure and Scripts

If you're just starting, learn structure. Save the Cat. 8-sequence. Hallmark's 9-Act. Then write a lot of scripts in a lot of genres. Get feedback, embrace criticism, and use contests if they help you grow—but don't rely on them as your career ladder.

At the end of the day, your "structure" is persistence. That's the one formula no writer can skip.

"Every writer needs inventory. Specs are your store window."

CHAPTER 4
Is my script any good?
Getting the exposure

Ranking the Contests

I'll admit it: I'm a contest junkie. Or maybe WAS. For someone who's not a gambler, I sure spent years feeding scripts into contests the way other people feed slot machines. The high was the same—the little dopamine hit when you saw your name on a list. Sometimes it was just "Quarterfinalist," but to me, it felt like winning the lottery.

And here's the thing: contests still matter. Like it or not, managers and producers want to know if your script has "placed." So after two decades of chasing validation and lessons learned the hard way, here's my personal ranking of contests and fellowships—the ones worth your money, time, and sanity.

The Nicholl Fellowship in Screenwriting

The gold standard. Run by the Academy of Motion Picture Arts and Sciences, it's the screenwriter's Oscars. Winning Nicholl means instant credibility, period.

But in 2025, the game changed. Nicholl no longer takes open submissions. You now have to apply through universities, labs, or filmmaker initiatives. For the rest of us, The Blacklist is the only doorway, and it's a pricey one. Between hosting fees and mandatory $100 evaluations, you're looking at $200 just to TRY. And only 25 scripts make it through that portal.

When I entered years ago, I made it to the Quarterfinals with two scripts, LAST HAND and FIRST MAN. Out of 6,000 entries, I was in the top 320. That was a moment of pure pride.

Takeaway: Enter if you can swing the cost. Even Quarterfinalist status can turn heads. But don't fool yourself, it's a lottery ticket with better odds than Powerball, but not by much.

Austin Film Festival (AFF)

AFF is the "writers' festival," and it earns that title. It's more than a contest, it's a community. The first time I went, I felt like I'd found my tribe. The panels, the barbecue, the conversations in hotel lobbies—it's summer camp for screenwriters.

Their contest is solid, too. Multiple categories (features, pilots, podcasts), and they actually give you feedback. Even being a second rounder gets you bragging rights and discounts. I've been there with my scripts KIRA AND HENRY, and BLOOD MOON WOLF. The recognition plus the networking made it worth every penny.

Takeaway: Enter if you value connections as much as accolades. The script might get you in the door, but the real prize is who you'll meet over beers.

PAGE International Screenwriting Awards

If Nicholl is art and Austin is community, PAGE is business. This contest is laser-focused on commercial appeal. High concept? Marketable? This is where those scripts shine.

They break it down by genre, which I love. My thriller isn't being judged against someone's rom-com. And the prizes aren't bad either—$25,000 grand prize plus $1,000 for each Gold winner.

Takeaway: Enter if your script is polished, pitchable, and ready for Hollywood.

Fellowships: Brutal but Worth It

Fellowships are contests' smarter, tougher cousins. They're usually free to enter, but the price tag is sweat equity—essays, interviews, recommendations, rewrites. Brutal. But the payoff? Career-changing.

- **NBC Writers Program** – 8 months of bootcamp and mentorship. A pipeline straight into staffing.

- **Disney DET Program** – practically guarantees you a staff writer spot if you get in.

- **Paramount Writers Program** – exec mentors and mock writers' rooms.

- **Native American Media Alliance Fellowship (NAMA)** – my holy grail. I applied four times, got in twice. It didn't pay cash, but it gave me confidence, craft, and community. It turned me into a TV writer.

This year, I threw my YA pilots WILMA WALLABY and KIRA AND HENRY into the Disney DET Program. Fingers crossed.

Takeaway: Enter every fellowship you qualify for. They're harder than contests, but the rewards can reshape your career.

Hosting Platforms

Where do your scripts "live" while they wait to be discovered?
Here are the big players:

- **Coverfly** – My personal favorite (RIP). Easy submissions, rankings, Red List glory. Gone in 2025, sadly.

- **The Blacklist** – Expensive, inconsistent, but now unavoidable thanks to Nicholl.

- **Stage 32** – Classes, pitches, networking. My lifeline during COVID. It's even how I met Alexia.

- **InkTip** – Old school but dependable. Their producer leads are still useful.

- **ISA** – Affordable, with gigs that sometimes surprise you. My WILMA WALLABY script found new life here.

Takeaway: Don't scatter yourself across everything. Pick one or two platforms and stick with them.

My Results

Here's the truth: I made 129 submissions in two years on Coverfly. I spent a small fortune. But I also made finals, hit the Red List, and most importantly, won the Native American Media Alliance Fellowship.

So yes, contests drained my bank account, but they forced me to write, to polish, and to face rejection until it didn't sting so badly.
Would I do it again? Probably. But these days, I'm more strategic. My 2025 mantra is taped above my desk: NO MORE CONTESTS! *(But ask me again next year.)*

CHAPTER 5
Assembling the right team and investing in yourself

Producers and Managers Who Ask for Money

People will tell you that if a manager, agent, or producer wants money to read your script or "work with you," then you should run. Fast. And that's good advice, for the most part.

But here's the nuance: after you DO land a manager, there will be expenses. Not shady "pay-to-play" fees, but practical investments like script coverage. Feedback is essential if you want your script to survive in the real world. I learned quickly that a good reader is worth their weight in gold. With the right notes, you don't just polish a script—you save yourself from sending out a dud that will haunt you forever.

When I signed with Alexia, we brought in Heidi, a professional reader. Thanks to that process, I now have several scripts sitting pretty at "Recommend" status, others at solid "Consider," and one unforgettable "Pass" that taught me humility.
The important thing? That "Pass" never went out the door. Because in this business, you only get one shot at a first impression.

Getting a Manager or Agent

A lot of emerging writers think landing an agent means Hollywood riches and development deals falling from the sky. I hate to be the truth-teller here, but unless your last name is Coppola, that's not how it works.

At the Austin Film Festival, I met Larry Postel, a Dallas screenwriter with no representation—yet he had four specs bought and produced since 2020. His secret? Smart, targeted queries. Larry wrote low-budget, limited-location scripts (the kind indie producers dream about), and he researched who could actually make those films.

Meanwhile, I blasted queries to producers and managers who weren't the right fit for my Cherokee lore-inspired scripts— and got crickets. Not even polite rejections. That's when I realized I needed more than persistence. I needed guidance. That's what ultimately led me to pursue management: not as a golden ticket, but as a partnership to shape my career.

Marketing & Writing Tools

Once you've rewritten your script into oblivion, gotten coverage, placed in contests, and have something ready to go, it's time to market your "inventory." That means learning to pitch.

I'm a former stutterer, so pitching terrified me. But preparation is everything. I started with written pitches—one-sheets, loglines, flyers—and then worked up to verbal pitching. My first live pitch at the Austin Film Festival? I survived, even got applause. Proof you CAN train yourself out of fear.

Today, I never write a script without writing the pitch first. Why? Because a script is a product, and if you can't pitch it, it's not ready. I write YA novels to express myself. I write screenplays to sell.

Pitch Decks and Lookbooks

The next step is visual. Pitch decks are your calling card—a way to show tone, style, and marketability at a glance. A strong deck can make the difference between "thanks, but no thanks" and "send me the script."

If you want to see a professional example, you can sneak a peek at the deck for my project LAST WOMAN, on my website. That deck, in fact, was what caught Alexia's attention and led to our partnership.

Lookbooks take it even further, a glossy catalogue that managers and sales agents use at film markets like Cannes or AFM. They're not cheap, but they're essential for presenting projects to international buyers.

Tools I Lean On

- **Canva** – My secret weapon for mock-ups and draft decks. User-friendly, with AI that helps me visualize ideas quickly.

- **Squarespace** – Clean, simple website design. I use it to host my writing portfolio and publishing projects.

- **Google Docs** – Ideal for collaboration (like this book with Alexia). Drafts, outlines, synopses—it all lives here.

- **AI (Claude, ChatGPT, Gemini)** – Great for brainstorming, research, or mock blurbs. But let's be clear: AI can't replace the human heart of storytelling. Only a writer can deliver that.

Social Media & Presence

I once thought social media didn't matter for screenwriters. But publishers, producers, and even contest judges are often curious about your presence. I joined SCBWI, built a small online platform, and today, my YouTube channel is approaching 100,000 views.

But here's the truth: in screenwriting, you're not judged by how many followers you have. You're judged on two things:

1. Can you write?

2. Are you easy to work with?

It's that simple. Nobody buys a ticket because Aaron Sorkin wrote it. They buy it because Spielberg or Gerwig directed it. And that's the beauty of this path—you can build a career as a screenwriter without being a household name.

CHAPTER 6
The BIG picture- no pun intended

What Kind of Screenwriter Do You Want to Be?

I thought the software industry was tough. Our clients were car dealers, and I used to joke, *"getting a car dealer interested in technology is harder than getting nuns into pornography."* (My apologies to my cousin Sister Frances and to my college advisor, Sister Cordele—may she rest in peace. Maybe that joke is what killed her!)

Turns out, Hollywood is tougher. The entertainment industry presents unique challenges and opportunities for writers. There are plenty of not-so-nice people, and as you try to carve out your space, you'll be asked to work for free—treatments, outlines, even full scripts. This is where the Writers Guild of America (WGA) comes in, providing protections, standards, and at least the hope of fair compensation.

To build a sustainable career, you need to understand both the creative AND the business sides. Networking is vital; relationships lead to opportunities in TV and film. But sooner or later, you'll face the question: DO I WANT TO BE A TV WRITER, A FEATURE WRITER, OR BOTH?

TV Writers

The difference between writing for television and film isn't just page count. A half-hour comedy is about 28 pages, a one-hour drama 45 pages. But multiply that by a season—ten or fifteen episodes—and you're writing the equivalent of three or four features.

TV writing is about LOCATION, LOCATION, LOCATION: the writer's room. Picture 9 to 15 writers around a table, debating arcs and character beats. I experienced this environment during my Native American Media Alliance Fellowships in 2023. It's not just about writing; it's reading other people's drafts, giving notes, and yes—talking endlessly about the writing.

Roles in the writer's room are tiered. At the top sits the showrunner, part creative visionary, part traffic cop. Below them are upper-level writers—executive producers and co-EPs—who help steer direction. Mid-levels (story editors, staff with credits) do much of the heavy lifting. At the entry level are staff writers, often fresh out of fellowships. They take notes, fetch coffee, and hope someone throws them a bone so they can earn a script credit.

It's collaborative, fast, and demanding. Deadlines are brutal, and shows are often still being written as episodes are shooting. It's a bit like working in the ER, if you can't handle pressure, TV may not be your lane.

The WGA Strike of 2023

In May 2023, 11,000 writers went on strike against the AMPTP (the major studios and streamers). It lasted five months, the longest in Hollywood history. Why? Writers were tired of stagnant pay, weak streaming residuals, and the looming threat of AI.

Some facts:

- Weekly writer-producer pay in 2019 was DOWN 23% from 2014, adjusted for inflation.

- Streaming shows pay far less residuals than traditional TV.

- Studios were raking in record profits while writers in LA and New York struggled to pay rent.

The new deal, reached in October 2023, delivered big wins:

- Higher minimums (up 5–15%).

- Better streaming residuals tied to production budgets.

- A ban on AI being used to write or rewrite scripts.

- Compensation if scripts are used to train AI.

But it came at a cost: billions lost in the LA economy, tens of thousands of crews out of work, and entire series cancelled or gutted. STRANGER THINGS, HOUSE OF THE DRAGON, SEVERANCE, and ONLY MURDERS IN THE BUILDING— all delayed. CBS even axed TRUE LIES, the show my mentor Kris Crenwelge had landed after winning the Disney Fellowship.

For studios, the strike became a convenient excuse to trim expensive projects. The cruel irony? Writers fought for their fair share, but the strike gave executives cover to slash the very shows providing jobs.

Feature Film Screenwriters

After twenty years, I discovered my true love: writing features, especially book adaptations. Writing alone, building worlds, structuring a two-hour story—that's my happy place. Not for everyone, but it works for me.

Feature writing is more solitary. You collaborate with producers and rewrite endlessly, but the first draft is you versus the blank page. Unlike TV, where characters evolve over years, features demand a complete arc in under 120 pages. Every scene matters. Dialogue has to be sharp, but film is visual, and audiences want moments, set pieces, spectacle.

If you thrive on collaboration and long-form arcs, TV might be your fit. If you crave control and love complete stories, features may be your path. Or, like me, you might straddle both. My background as a programmer trained me to pivot fast—pilot, feature, YA novel, even non-fiction—depending on what's urgent.

Genre & Brand

Your "brand" is the sum of your voice, your strengths, and your professional style. For me, it's simple:

- I'm **fast** (I type as fast as I think).

- I'm **good** (trained, educated, with life experience).

- I'm **cheap** (cue Alexia cringing). I don't chase money; I chase getting things produced.

My sweet spot is adaptations, especially grounded sci-fi. So, what does "grounded sci-fi" mean? Unlike STAR WARS or GUARDIANS OF THE GALAXY, grounded sci-fi stays rooted in plausibility:

1. Realistic science and technology.

2. Relatable settings (soccer fields, small towns, not galaxies far, far away).

3. Near-future scenarios (a decade or two out, not millennia).

4. Real consequences.

Think THE MARTIAN (yes, with my darling Matt Damon) or MINORITY REPORT. My scripts—TECHNICALLY SOCCER, LAST WOMAN, RUNAWAY CRICKET—play in that sandbox.

But here's the bigger point: FIND YOUR GENRE, THEN BUILD YOUR BRAND AROUND IT. Aaron Sorkin moved from plays (A FEW GOOD MEN) to features (THE AMERICAN PRESIDENT) to TV (THE WEST WING). Me? I've dabbled in all of it—screenplays, pilots, plays, books. My through-line is adaptation. Yours might be horror, comedy, or romance. Whatever it is, own it.

CHAPTER 7
What's your story worth?

"Imagination will often carry us to worlds that never were, but without it, we go nowhere." — Carl Sagan

My first year as a screenwriter landed me two adaptation jobs: HIJACKED and JAKE & CLARA. Both taught me the same hard lesson—books and movies are different animals.

When I read HIJACKED, it was clear the book was too sprawling for a two-hour movie. It spent chapters diving into each pilot's backstory, plus the hijacker's motivations. Great for a novel. For a film? Too much. So, I boiled it down: A DISGRUNTLED EMPLOYEE HIJACKS A PLANE. That's the movie. Trim the noise, stay on the action.

With JAKE & CLARA, the story wasn't about Jake—it was about Clara. She shoots him...and gets away with it! So, I shifted the focus, made Clara the main character, and built her arc around that act. That's the trick with adaptation: stop worrying about including EVERYTHING from the book. Instead, pick your character, pick their arc, and hang the story on that.

Learning from CONTACT

To sharpen my skills, I compared Carl Sagan's CONTACT with its film. What stood out? The book had a sprawling backstory, philosophy, multiple romances, and a team of travellers. The movie streamlined it all into one emotional journey—Ellie alone meeting the aliens, with a cleaner focus on faith versus science.

And here's the irony: CONTACT was first written as a screenplay, rejected, then turned into a novel, which became a bestseller, and only THEN circled back to Hollywood. Sometimes you have to write the book to get the film.

Protecting IP by Writing the Book

These days, I've done my own "Sagan shuffle." I wrote MAMA DALLAS AND AUGIE as books after starting them as screenplays, and I'm plotting MACHIAVELLI'S PRINCESS, based on a screenplay by Alexia's mother. Even THE LAST POE became a novel after Heidi adapted it from a script I co-wrote.

Why go backward, from script to book? Protection. Writing the book establishes the IP and sets up potential sequels. It's armor.
When I pitched BLOOD MOON WOLF on Stage 32, a Paramount+ producer told me the concept was fun—but studios in sci-fi/fantasy want existing IP. So I rewrote it as a YA novel. That way, I had a story AND a product that proved its value.

Why Hollywood Loves IP

Studios like IP because it's safer:

- **Built-in fans** – Awareness before the trailer even drops.

- **Proof of concept** – A bestseller or hit game shows the story works.

- **Franchise potential** – Sequels, spin-offs, and universes = $$$.

That's why we see HARRY POTTER, THE HUNGER GAMES, THE SOCIAL NETWORK, THE LEGO MOVIE, and even PIRATES OF THE CARIBBEAN (from a theme park ride!)

Reverse-Engineering IP

Some writers create "reverse IP"—turning a script into a book, comic, or podcast first to make it more marketable. Derek Kolstad did this with JOHN WICK, building a mythology so rich it felt like pre-existing IP.

And yes, original hits still break through: EVERYTHING EVERYWHERE ALL AT ONCE, GET OUT, A QUIET PLACE, KNIVES OUT. But if you've got a great idea, think about protecting it in book form too.

Takeaway

Adaptation isn't about copying—it's about focus. Pick the character, the arc, the story that matters, and trim the rest. And if you're building something new? Consider protecting it by creating IP. Because in today's Hollywood, a book, a comic, or even a podcast can be the difference between a "pass" and a greenlight.

CHAPTER 8
Will the real producer please stand up?

"Producing is the hardest job because the producer is the first one on the movie, and the last one to leave." — Brian Grazer

During my Native American Media Alliance Fellowship, almost everyone wanted to direct or produce. Me? I was in the 1% that didn't. I'm a writer. That has always been my dream, and I feel like it's a miracle that at my age, I get to live it.

Still, I had to ask myself: should I be looking at producing or directing too? Many of you may be wondering the same thing: WHAT DOES PRODUCING REALLY INVOLVE?

The Producer Puzzle

On television, "producer" can mean many things. Executive Producer, Co-Executive Producer, Supervising Producer, Co-Producer, Associate Producer, Segment Producer, Line Producer, the list goes on. Titles reflect both seniority and responsibilities:

- **Executive Producer** – often the showrunner, the ultimate creative authority.

- **Co-Executive Producer** – senior writers who run the writers' room.

- **Supervising Producer** – veterans guiding episode writers.

- **Producer/Co-Producer** – writers moving up the ladder, adding scripts and notes.

- **Associate Producer** – often the junior support in writing and production.

- **Segment Producer** – producing a specific field or episodic segment.

- **Line Producer** – the one who wrangles budgets, schedules, and logistics.

Film producers, meanwhile, wear looser hats. A "producer" might be an investor, someone who develops and sells packages, or the hands-on person shepherding the movie from start to finish.

The Producers Guild of America (PGA) helps define these roles and protects the integrity of the "Produced By" credit. It's also a marker of credibility, community, and standards. Alexia is a PGA producer herself.

Why Not Direct?

If producing is tough, directing is even tougher. Directors are visionaries who translate the script into a living, breathing story on screen. They cast, collaborate with every department, shape performances, and carry the project from prep through post. It's an enormous responsibility and, frankly, one I have no desire for.

As Orson Welles said, *"the whole eloquence of cinema is achieved in the editing room."* That's directing in a nutshell. Vital, visionary, and absolutely not for me. I'd rather not be the goalie, the pitcher, or the president. I'll happily cheer from the sidelines as a writer.

My Detour Before Writing

I didn't always dare to call myself a screenwriter. Twenty years ago, I stood at a crossroads: leap into writing or stick to financial security. Then tragedy struck, and my husband and I stepped up to raise our four granddaughters. I chose stability.

I became a computer consultant, known in the auto industry as a "fixer." I built software for car dealerships, wrote articles, gave seminars, and became a name in that world. At the time, if you said "Digital Dealer," chances are you also knew me.

That detour gave me security—but it delayed my writing dream. If I could go back, I'd tell myself: work a few more years at that CFO salary, THEN jump into screenwriting. Instead, I took the long way around. But the long way gave me experience, grit, and eventually the freedom to write full-time.

What I've Learned

Looking back, I realize the industry doesn't just need great producers or directors—it needs writers who know how to pitch, package, and protect their work. If I had someone like Alexia twenty years ago, I'd have avoided so many mistakes. She taught me to market myself, to create a brand, and to always keep moving forward.

Today, I measure my success in persistence and partnership. My biggest assets have been:

1. **Finding Alexia** as my manager and producer ally.

2. **Not giving up.**

I like to say I'm "almost famous"—and happily so.

Writers, Agents, and Managers

For those of you wondering: agents and managers are not the same thing.

- **Agents** sell your work. They pitch to studios, negotiate deals, and focus on transactions. They're licensed, commission 10%, and usually handle big client lists.

- **Managers** guide your career. They develop your voice, help with scripts, strategy, branding, and sometimes produce. They're more personal, more long-term.

Many writers eventually have both, but in the beginning, you might only need one. For me, Alexia has been that guiding hand. I also have my eye on a literary agent for my YA and Middle-Grade novels. Tools like Query Tracker help me target the right ones.

My Future Plans

I'm not a producer-writer. I don't want to direct. I just want to write stories and see them made. Right now, I've got one project in production, another close to funding, and one heading toward Hallmark. I'm also focusing on getting my Cherokee novels into schools and libraries through a literary agent.

And I'll keep pitching. Because that's what writers do: we keep putting stories into the world.

Final Words

I once read this advice from Jonathan Silverman, quoting John Lithgow: *"Don't ever get too hot, and don't get too cold. Just kind of stay lukewarm. And you're going to have a lovely, lovely career."*
I think that describes me perfectly—I'm happy lukewarm. Not chasing every fire, not frozen by fear, just steady, present, and writing.

If you've come this far in this book, you're probably about to start your own journey. Learn from my detours, take the leap earlier if you can, and trust that with persistence and the right guidance, you'll find your way.

I call myself a huge success, not because I'm rich or famous, but because I'm still here, writing every day.
And if you need inspiration on the way? Read my blog: sandijerome.blogspot.com. Because if I can do this, so can you.

Closing Thoughts: Your Heart's Calling Awaits

As you close this book, I invite you to pause. Take a deep breath. Let everything you've read—the wisdom, the struggles, the victories—sink into your heart. Each story has been more than just an interview; it's been a mirror. A reminder that those who succeed in Hollywood—and beyond—are not born with certainty. They wrestle with fear, rejection, doubt, and the temptation to quit. Yet, they persist. They discover what Reverend Beckwith calls our "one of one" nature—that singular spark no one else can bring.

From Blair Underwood's reminder that PASSION IS THE COMPASS... to the Parlaplanides Brothers' relentless pursuit of their vision... to DeeDee Pfeiffer's courage to transform pain into purpose—every voice in these pages affirms the same truth: success belongs to those who dare to keep going.

The Thread That Connects Us All

Evan Spiliotopoulos reminded us that "character is plot." Just as screenplays are built on choices, so are our lives. Every setback you've faced is not the end—it's just Act Two, building toward your Act Three.

Jonathan Silverman's advice to stay "lukewarm" may sound counterintuitive, but it carries a deep truth: fall in love with the process, not the outcome. Because joy in the journey is what sustains us when applause fades and rejection knocks.

Keith Mitchell, Jon Paul Crimi, and Reverend Beckwith shared a different kind of wisdom—that success is also about stillness, intention, and the courage to be present. They remind us that the inner world fuels the outer one.

And from RB Botto, we learned one of the most practical lessons: YOU ARE THE CEO OF YOU, INC. Every connection, every pitch, every choice builds your brand.

My Personal Takeaways for You

Having walked my own unpredictable path through this industry, here's what I want to leave you with:

- **Success isn't linear.** I arrived in America as a teenager with my single mother, $5,000 in our pockets, and no guarantees. Decades later, I can tell you: persistence always outlives rejection.

- **Your story is your superpower.** Don't dilute it. Hollywood doesn't need another copy; it needs your unfiltered originality.

- **Relationships matter more than deals.** The "inner circle" isn't a secret club; it's built one authentic connection at a time.

- **Protect your energy.** No career is worth losing yourself. Do the inner work, honor your boundaries, and keep your joy intact.

- **Timing is divine.** You're not behind. You're not late. You're right where you need to be—becoming who you're meant to become.

Why Not You?

As Dimitris Logothetis so perfectly put it: "WHY NOT YOU?" Why not be the one to get the deal, to tell the story, to leave the legacy? Every person you've read about in this book once sat exactly where you are now—uncertain, hopeful, wondering if their dream was too far out of reach.

The truth? The industry needs you. Your voice. Your vision. Your ripple.

So, here's my call to you: close this book, take a breath, and take one bold step forward. Write the page. Send the email. Call the contact. Submit the script. Start. Because the heart of show business has never been about red carpets or contracts— it's about the fire inside you to tell stories that matter.

Hollywood doesn't belong to the chosen few. It belongs to the brave.

And now—it belongs to you.

With love, courage, and belief in your dreams,

Alexia Melocchi

Beverly Hills, 2025

Sandi's Recommended Toolbox

Essential Screenwriting Books:
- **Save the Cat!** by Blake Snyder – The Bible of beat sheets. If you only read one book, make it this one. (And yes, Final Draft has a template for it.)
- **The Writer's Journey** by Christopher Vogler –Based on Joseph Campbell's Hero's Journey. Great for mythic structure and character arcs.
- **Story** by Robert McKee – Dense but brilliant. If you like lectures that make you feel guilty for every cliché you've ever written, this is it.
- **Your Screenplay Sucks!** by William M. Akers – Because sometimes blunt advice is exactly what you need.
- **The TV Writer's Workbook** by Ellen Sandler – Practical advice from a sitcom veteran.
- **The Hollywood Standard** by Christopher Riley – Formatting rules you *must* know.
- **Adventures in the Screen Trade** by William Goldman – Honest, funny, and essential perspective.
- **The Business of Adaptation** by Linda Seger – A how-to manual for turning books into screenplays.
- **An Insider's Secret: Mastering the Hollywood Path** by Alexia Melocchi – Yes, my manager wrote it. Yes, I'm biased. But it's the best crash course in how Hollywood REALLY works.

Podcasts Worth Your Time:
- **Scriptnotes** (John August & Craig Mazin) – Craft + business with wit and honesty.
- **The Writers Panel** – In-depth interviews with working writers.

- **The Treatment** (Elvis Mitchell) – Conversations on film, culture, and creativity.
- **The Heart of Show Business** (Alexia Melocchi) – Insightful industry conversations.
- **The Screenwriting Life** – Practical tips and real talk for writers.
- **Children of Tendu** – Inside the TV writer's room.
- **OnWriting** (WGA East) – Writers on their process and projects.

Screenwriting Software:
- **Final Draft** – Industry standard. Expensive, but widely used for collaboration.
- **Fade In** – Affordable, sleek, excellent for solo writing.
- **WriterDuet** – Great for collaboration, especially TV writers' rooms.
- **Highland 2** – Minimalist, distraction-free writing.
- **Scrivener** – Ideal for adaptations or big, research-heavy projects.
- **Movie Magic Screenwriter** – Old guard, still useful for stage plays.

Tip: Pick the tool that keeps you writing. The software won't write the script—you will.

Screenwriting Contests & Fellowships:
- **Academy Nicholl Fellowships** – The gold standard. Industry attention guaranteed if you place.
- **Austin Film Festival** – Top-tier networking and a great creative community.
- **Page International** – Large, respected, competitive.
- **Stage 32 Contests** – Smaller, niche categories, better odds.

- **ISA (International Screenwriters' Association)** – Affordable contests plus job boards.
- **Diversity Fellowships** (e.g., Native American Media Alliance) – Career-changing opportunities.

Coverage & Feedback:
- **Professional Coverage** – Invest in reputable readers. Always ask who's behind the notes.
- **Trusted Peers** – Script swaps are gold. If multiple people flag the same issue, it's real.
- **AI Tools** –
    - Callaia (used by studios & producers)
    - Prescene, RivetAI, ScriptReader.AI (fast, affordable feedback)
    - ChatGPT / Claude (useful for loglines, synopses, idea-testing—not for writing scripts for you).

Writing Habits & Productivity:
- **Treadmill Desk** – Write and stay healthy (5K steps + 10 pages = win).
- **Notebooks Everywhere** – Ideas vanish if you don't capture them.
- **Guard Your Quiet Hours** – Whether 4 AM or midnight, protect your peak focus time.
- **Contest Calendar** – Plan submissions early to avoid 11:59 PM panic.
- **Budget Tracking** – Contests, coverage, and festivals add up. Stay in control.

Pitching & Marketing Survival Kit

Pitch Materials
- One-Sheets – Logline, synopsis, and comps at a glance.
- Pitch Decks – A visual storytelling tool: part mood board, part movie poster.
- Lookbooks – For multi-project presentations at markets.

Tools
- Canva – Easy design for decks and visuals.
- Squarespace / Wix / WordPress – Build a clean online portfolio.
- Google Docs – Perfect for outlines and collaboration drafts.

Practice Habits
- Pitch before you write. If you can't sell it in a sentence, it's not ready.
- Record yourself, check pacing, tone, and clarity.
- Rehearse with a friend (or mirror) until confidence kicks in.

Reminder: A pitch isn't just selling, it's about clarity, confidence, and connection.

Industry & Career Resources:
- **So You Want to Be a Producer** by Lawrence Turman – Lessons from a Hollywood veteran.
- **The Hollywood Pitching Bible** by Douglas Eboch & Ken Aguado – Smart strategies for pitching.
- **PGA, WGA, DGA** – Learn the unions, protections, and career pathways.
- **The Blacklist** – Paid hosting and feedback (pricey but valuable).
- **Stage 32** – Networking, classes, contests, and pitching opportunities.

- **Query Tracker** – Database for literary agents (especially useful if you cross into publishing).

Pro Tips:
- Managers guide your career; agents sell your work. Know the difference.
- Producers are there from start to finish—decide if you want that responsibility.
- No one cares about your story as much as you do. Keep pitching.

Final Word

The best tool in your kit isn't software or contests or coverage. It's persistence. All the apps, books, and podcasts in the world won't matter if you don't put words on the page.

Find what keeps you writing—and stick with it.

Alexia's Toolbox

Podcasts That Inspire:

- **On Purpose** – Jay Shetty: Conversations on mindset, purpose, and personal growth.

- **The Mel Robbins Podcast** – Practical tools for courage, clarity, and confidence.

- **School of Greatness** – Lewis Howes: Success stories and strategies from world-class leaders.

- **Take Back Your Mind** – Michael Beckwith: Spiritual practices for presence and transformation.

- **The Heart of Show Business** – Alexia Melocchi: Industry insights and authentic conversations (yes, my own!).

Books That Shaped My Journey:

- **Hello, He Lied** by Linda Obst – Candid look inside the producing world.

- **So You Want to Be a Producer** by Lawrence Turman – Timeless wisdom from a Hollywood veteran.

- **The 48 Laws of Power** by Robert Greene – Strategy, influence, and human dynamics.

- **Save the Cat!** by Blake Snyder – The ultimate beat sheet bible for writers.

- **The Mailroom** by David Rensin – Gritty origin stories of Hollywood's power players.

- **Essentialism** by Greg McKeown – The disciplined pursuit of less but better.

- **The Illusion of Money** by Kyle Cease – Mindset reset on wealth, worth, and creativity.

- **The 12 Week Year** by Brian Moran – Productivity and goal setting redefined.

- **Awaken the Giant Within** by Tony Robbins – Personal mastery and empowered decision-making.

- **Hook Point** by Brendan Kane – Grabbing attention in a 3-second world.

Sign up for exclusive private coaching with Alexia to prepare for what could potentially become the most pivotal meeting of your life.
Make sure you're fully equipped and primed for success.

POWER HOUR- CREATIVE COACHING

https://www.alexia-melocchi.com/coaching

LET'S CONNECT!

www.alexia-melocchi.com
https://alexiamelocchi.com/
www.littlestudiofilms.com
https://www.youtube.com/@AlexiaMelocchi/videos
https://www.instagram.com/alexiamelocchireal
https://www.tiktok.com/@alexiamelocchi

www.ingramcontent.com/pod-product-compliance
Lightning Source LLC
Chambersburg PA
CBHW060426130626

46555CB00005B/2233